I0807830

Contents

The Rocky Road to the Fourth International, 1933-38[1]

by George Breitman

One of the good things about Trotsky's *History of the Russian Revolution* is that along with the clash of hostile class forces in that revolution it presents the disputes and struggles that took place inside the monarchy, the bourgeoisie, the petty bourgeoisie, and the proletariat, and the parties that spoke or tried to speak for them. Most valuable of all is the story it tells about what went on inside the Bolshevik Party—not only its decisions and actions, its strengths and victories, but also its hesitations and uncertainties, its mistakes and weaknesses, and how it resolved them through debate and conflict.

Believing that to be the best method for studying revolutionary history, and hoping that that aspect of Trotsky's *History* will serve as a model when the history of the Fourth International is written, I offer the following as a contribution to the study of an important segment of that history, the five-year period that ended in the foundation of the Fourth International in September 1938. This was the period that Trotsky called the second and final phase of the "prehistory" of the Fourth International.

Internationalism was at the heart of the Marxist movement from its inception. When their *Communist Manifesto* called on the workers of the world to unite, Marx and Engels did not mean this in a merely rhetorical or symbolical sense—they meant that revolutionary workers must build an international organization as well as national parties—and when the opportunity arose they helped to organize and lead the First International. Nobody who claimed to be a Marxist in the 1930s disputed the necessity of a Marxist International, although there were differences about the kind that was needed. This was before Stalin dissolved the Communist International during World War II, that is, before Stalin decreed that an international party had become outmoded, a view that is still championed by all the branches and offshoots of Stalinism today.

So in 1933 the critical problem facing revolutionaries was not whether to have or build an international Marxist party but a related though separate question: What do revolutionaries do when an international party becomes corrupt or degenerates and departs from its originally revolutionary principles and practices? Do they remain members of such an international trying to correct its course or do they, at a certain point, decide that such efforts are hopeless, break with the old International and try to build a new one?

A certain body of experience had already accumulated around this question. In the 1870s Marx and Engels agreed to the dissolution of the First International they had founded rather than let it fall into the hands of the anarchists. This cleared the path after Marx's death for the formation of the new Second International, which united the Marxists of the world and played a generally progressive role during the next quarter of a century. In 1914 Lenin called for a new International because the Second had betrayed Marxism by supporting the imperialists in World War I. This orientation guided the Bolsheviks and other internationalists through the war and the Russian revolution and led, more than four years after Lenin's first call, to the foundation of the Third or Communist International.

These developments supplied what might be called precedents for the decision that presented itself in 1933, but of course precedents alone could not determine a decision of such gravity: the chief criterion was objective necessity. And that was the criterion that prevailed at the meeting of the International Left Opposition's executive committee in France in August 1933, which voted to start work toward the formation of a new revolutionary International. It was undoubtedly the single most important decision in the 55-year history of our movement.[2]

For ten years, since 1923, the Left Opposition had been working to reform the Communist International and return it to the path of Leninism and the revolutionary internationalist principles developed under Lenin's leadership at the first four congresses of the Comintern. Although expelled from the Comintern and its affiliates, the Left Oppositionists regarded themselves as a faction of the Comintern, demanding reinstatement and disclaiming any intention of becoming an independent movement in competition with the Comintern.

But Hitler came to power early in 1933, not only because of the cowardice of the Social Democratic and union leaders but also because of the policies of the Stalinized Comintern, which fought bitterly and successfully to prevent any united front struggle against the Nazis. And in the months that followed, the executive committee of the Comintern, refusing to acknowledge any responsibility for the fascist annihilation of the powerful German workers' movement, unanimously reaffirmed the policies that had produced the German catastrophe. This reaffirmation convinced Trotsky and other leaders of the Left Opposition that the Comintern's degeneration had passed the point where its reform was any longer possible, that it was finished as a revolutionary force, and that a new International to replace it was the most urgent need of the international working class.

It was a striking example of simultaneous continuity and change. The principles—of Leninism—remained the same, but in order to promote and realize those principles it now became necessary to radically change the movement's orientation, organizational character and tactics. Previously, the major, the virtually exclusive work of our movement had been the preparation and dissemination of propaganda directed at the Communist parties, their ranks and their periphery, seeking to persuade them to change their policies so that the Communist parties could become capable of leading proletarian revolutions. Now the axis of our work was fundamentally changed. We ourselves were going to undertake the responsibility of building the Leninist international and parties—not alone of course, but together with other revolutionary forces, including those that could still be won from the CPs. Propaganda would continue to be essential, but its form would have to be altered and widened because it would be aimed at non-CP as well as CP audiences, and it would have to be combined with work in the labor and mass movements and with other independent activities to build the cadres of the new Leninist parties.

To appreciate the magnitude, the audacity, and the difficulties

1. An abridged version of this talk was given at a socialist educational conference in Oberlin, Ohio, on August 5, 1978.

2. The ILO's August 1933 resolution is translated into English for the first time as Appendix A.

of this undertaking requires an effort of historical imagination and some knowledge of the state of the Left Opposition at that time.

For ten years its members had been recruited around the idea that a Leninist faction in the CPs was needed, not a new party; they had been educated around this idea after being recruited; and most of their activity had been devoted to spreading this idea among their contacts. *Faction—not party* thus had the status almost of a tradition. So it might be expected that there would be a strong psychological resistance to the new orientation. But in fact it was surprisingly small and brief. A dissident group split away in France but it probably would have split over another issue if this one hadn't come along, and here and there individual members could not adjust to the turn and dropped out. Opposition was so minimal that the leaders felt it was possible to make this momentous change without holding an international conference.

The near-unanimity testifies to a relatively high level of political consciousness among the members of the Left Opposition, who had tried to influence the outcome of the fight against fascism in Germany before it triumphed and who grasped the main implications of the worst defeat the worker's movement had ever suffered. And it testifies to the exceptional authority held by Trotsky, whose arguments in favor of the new orientation seemed irrefutable to the members. But it may also have reflected an inadequate awareness of the towering obstacles that lay ahead, which nobody could have foreseen in all their concreteness.

One of the principal assets of the Left Opposition has already been mentioned—the fact that its members were better educated ideologically and politically than any other tendency of the period. But on the other side, it was a small, weak, and poor movement.

An international conference in February 1933 had been attended by representatives of the Opposition from eleven countries: ten in Europe[3], and the United States. The Soviet and Italian sections were organizations in exile, and most of the German leaders had to go into exile after Hitler's victory. By that time the Opposition in the Soviet Union no longer existed as a functioning organization, its remaining supporters having been isolated, exiled or imprisoned by the Stalinist repression, cut off from each other as well as from Trotsky and the Opposition center abroad. The Greek and Spanish sections were the largest, each having over a thousand members. The other main sections had memberships averaging a few hundred, and many of the sections were smaller. Most of the sections were unable to publish regularly even a four-page weekly paper. One reason why an international conference was not held late in 1933 was the material poverty of the movement, which had held a conference in February and couldn't afford the expense of another so soon. In fact, the next international conference was not held until 1936.

Both the Second International and the Third International at this time had millions of members. There were two other international groupings on the left—the International Communist Opposition or Right Opposition, which was led by Heinrich Brandler, and the loose centrist coalition of left Social Democrats and dissident Communist tendencies expelled from the Comintern for opposing the ultraleftism of the Stalinist "third period," which later came to be known as the London Bureau. Both of these two groups in 1933 had affiliates with memberships many times larger than the maximum of four or five thousand then adhering to the Left Opposition. The mightiest movements always begin small, so smallness is not a sin, provided it is not persisted in. But smallness is also never a virtue or an advantage for those whose aim is to win a majority to change the world.

Besides its small numbers, the Left Opposition had the handicap of an unfavorable class composition, most of its sections having a large percentage of petty-bourgeois elements, intellectuals, and students. This too is not uncommon in the early stages of workers' movements but invariably creates critical problems for them. In addition, many of the members were immigrants who were not well acquainted with the country where they lived or its labor movement. Most of the members were young and had little previous political or organizational experience. Some had had prior experience only in the Communist parties in the years when they were being Stalinized, where they were seriously miseducated on many questions.

The leaders of the sections tended to be a little older and more experienced. Some had roots in the workers' movement extending back before the Russian revolution or World War I, and a few of the national leaderships, such as the Belgian and the American, had the important advantage of having worked together in the CPs instead of having met, so to speak, for the first time in the Left Opposition. But none of them had yet completely freed themselves of the concept that prevailed in the Comintern after Lenin and before it was completely subjugated by the Stalinist faction—namely, the concept that the revolutionary party is a federation of factions rather than a combat organization striving for political homogeneity and a collective leadership. Unprincipled factionalism and even cliquism frequently undermined efforts to achieve political and organizational stability in the national sections of the Opposition and their leading bodies.

Until 1933, the only international coordinating committee the Left Opposition had was the International Secretariat; in that year, it was supplemented by an executive committee, which was really only an enlarged IS. The composition of the IS was partly accidental because the national sections lacked money to send representative and authoritative members to serve at the center in Paris. Most of the IS members were young and its composition changed frequently, often as a result of factional changes in the national leaderships, especially in the French section. It had only one full-time staff member, the administrative secretary, the other members devoting most of their time to the work of their own sections. All in all, the independent authority of the IS in this period was never very high.

Our greatest asset in the thirties was the leadership provided by Trotsky. In his person was represented direct continuity with the experiences of the Russian revolution, the long uphill struggles that preceded it, and the lessons of the Comintern in both Lenin's and Stalin's times. This continuity enabled the Left Opposition to escape most of the ruinous mistakes and false starts that plague movements starting out from scratch. His authority—moral, political, and theoretical—towered over that of all the other Opposition leaders. He knew, better than anyone else, about the shortcomings of the IS, but he also knew, as any good branch organizer does, that you have to work with the forces available and not reject them because they are less than ideal or perfect. Trotsky had an unshakable belief in the capacity of the workers to free themselves from class exploitation and oppression, given adequate leadership, and the conviction, which never left him, that the working class vanguard was capable of forging such a leadership. These were the sources of both his patience with others and his own unceasing activism even when he was hemmed in like a prisoner in a cell. And so he worked with the members of the IS and the national leaderships, trying to educate them in the methods of Marxism and principled politics, to help them meet their responsibilities as revolutionary cadres and provide collective leadership for the whole movement. It was often frustrating work because all of them were operating under murderous pressures—the pressures of isolation and an unending series of defeats and setbacks, the pressures of imperialism and of Stalinism, repression of every kind, the spread of fascism, the poverty and demoralization resulting from mass unemployment, and much more—and most of the leading peoples in the thirties

3. Germany, France, Britain, Belgium, Greece, Spain, Bulgaria, Switzerland, Italy, and the USSR. Other Oppositionist groups existed—in China, South Africa, Latin America, central Europe, etc.—but were not represented at this conference.

were gone from the movement by the end of World War II. Trotsky by himself could not compensate for unfavorable objective conditions or IS leadership weaknesses, but he could and did limit their impact on the work of the movement, sometimes decisively.

The first results of the August 1933 decision to work for a new International were quite encouraging.

A week later there was an international conference in Paris of the centrist groups in and around the London Bureau, and the Left Oppositionists participated in order to raise the call for a new International and win allies around this call, which came to be known as the Declaration of Four. Trotsky had pointed to the inevitability of ferment in the radical movement as the lessons of the German catastrophe sank in, and to the likelihood that this would result in the emergence or strengthening of left wing tendencies inside the centrist and Social Democratic organizations. This was confirmed at the Paris conference where three national groups joined with the Left Opposition in signing the Declaration of Four.[4] Two of these groups soon changed their minds about a new International but the third, a Dutch organization led by the veteran communist Henricus Sneevliet, joined the Left Opposition as its Dutch section and he himself became a member of its executive committee, playing an important role in it during the following five years.

Shortly after the Sneevliet group's adherence, the International Left Opposition changed its name to the International Communist League (ICL), the name by which we were known internationally until 1936.

The new orientation had healthy effects in several of the sections. In France it motivated the Opposition's youth group to initiate serious fraction work inside the Socialist Party's youth group, which led to valuable results a year later. In the United States it provided a favorable climate for the resolution of an internal crisis between the supporters of James P. Cannon on one side and of Max Shachtman and Martin Abern on the other that had crippled the American section for three years. Thanks to the help of Trotsky and the IS, the old differences were put aside and there ensued a period of fruitful collaboration between Cannon and Shachtman that lasted through the founding conference of the International, in 1938, making the American section the strongest in the movement and the one that went farthest along the road of transforming itself from a propagandist group to a workers' party of mass action.

But not all the results were positive. I have mentioned that a small group split from the French section when the new line was adopted, but its members had been on their way out for two years, and their departure was a blessing. More serious was the fact that behind the scenes they had the encouragement of an IS member in Paris, Witte of the Greek section.[5] When the IS and Trotsky called Witte to order, he quit, and under his influence the Greek section, the largest in the Opposition, also broke away from the ICL.

The political reasons for the split were not too clear at the time; the Greek leadership contended that only organizational principles were in contention. But soon after splitting from the ICL in 1934, they affiliated to the London Bureau, which was adamantly opposed to a new International. Objectively, it would appear, the split involved divergent views on the need for a Fourth International even though the Greek leaders never posed the issue that way before the split.

One of the London Bureau groups that attended the Paris conference was the centrist Independent Labour Party of Britain. The ILP delegates voted against the Declaration of Four but some of its leaders were interested enough to visit Trotsky in France to discuss perspectives. Because of these talks and his reading of the ILP press, Trotsky concluded that an important part of the ILP was in motion toward the left, and he proposed that the members of the year-old British section of the Left Opposition should enter the ILP in order to win support for the Fourth International perspective. The IS agreed with this proposal, and formally recommended it to the British section.

In what resembled a dress rehearsal for a much bigger debate over "entrism" a year later, the leaders of the British section, which had only 40 members and not much independent experience, responded with shock and indignation. What! Right on the heels of calling for a new International and new revolutionary parties, we should go into a miserable outfit like the ILP? Wasn't this in contradiction to the principle that the independence of the revolutionary party must be maintained at all times! Trotsky tried patiently to explain that 40 members were not yet a revolutionary party but only a nucleus for such a party, that the nucleus could expand only through organizational flexibility and tactical suppleness, that the nucleus could preserve its political independence by functioning as a disciplined fraction inside the ILP, and so on. But the sectarian formalists in the British leadership would not listen, and even though the entry proposal was only a recommendation, and not a command, they expelled a minority that favored entry and split away from the International Left Opposition. Later, most of them were to join the ILP but not as a revolutionary fraction of the Fourth Internationalist movement.

As these and other examples in 1933 and later show, merely adopting the new orientation, although necessary, was not sufficient. Cadres in the revolutionary movement cannot be measured only by the good resolutions they vote for or adopt. What counts even more is how they implement those resolutions. Almost everybody in 1933 voted for a new International. But many did not really understand what they were voting for or how to carry it out in practice, and others changed their minds along the way when they saw or felt the immensity of the task.

At the end of 1933 the four organizations that had signed the Declaration of Four held a conference to consider their next steps in elaborating a program for the future International and the areas of collaboration that could take place among the four organizations. It was held in Paris, and Trotsky was part of the ICL delegation. It was agreed to hold another conference six weeks later and to prepare programmatic documents for that, but the exchanges between the ICL representatives and those of the German and Dutch centrists were so sharp that the prospects did not look promising; in fact this was the last joint meeting of the Four, and the proposed February conference never took place.

I mention the conference mainly to call attention to the composition of the ICL delegation, whom I shall designate as the Eight, because they personify and illustrate some of the central problems and developments of the period. One, there was Trotsky. Two, Sneevliet, the leader of the new Dutch section. Three, Erwin Bauer, the leader of the German section, who was then administrative secretary of the IS. Four, Alfonso Leonetti, a founder of the Italian section. Five and six, Pierre Naville and Pierre Frank, founders of the French section. Seven, Leon Sedov, Trotsky's son, a leader of the movement in his own right. And eight, Rudolf Klement, Trotsky's German-language secretary and later administrative secretary of the IS.

These eight Europeans were not the entire leadership of the ICL at the end of 1933, but they included most of the central core.

4. The three were the Socialist Workers Party of Germany (SAP), the Independent Socialist Party of Holland (OSP), and the Revolutionary Socialist Party of Holland (RSP). The SAP was organized in 1931 after a left wing tendency was expelled from the German Social Democracy; although outlawed by the Nazis, it claimed over 10,000 members in 1933. The OSP originated in 1932 out of a left wing split from the Dutch Social Democracy, and had an estimated 4,000 members. The RSP was organized in 1929 after its leaders were expelled from the Dutch CP for opposing Stalinism; it had almost a thousand members.

5. The Archeo-Marxists were a tendency in the Greek CP that was expelled in 1924. After functioning as a propagandist group for some years, they became a serious competitor of the CP. They began to sympathize with the Left Opposition in 1930 and joined as its Greek section in 1932. Witte became a member of the IS the same year.

Sedov and Klement were both to be murdered by the GPU in 1938, in the months before the International's founding conference. As our narrative continues, we will take note of what happened to the other six.

Pulling together the forces of the Fourth International was not only and it was not mainly an organizational problem. It was a political problem primarily. When we were a faction of the Comintern, it sufficed to criticize the errors of the Comintern. But an independent International, if its existence is to be justified and if it is to attract people who will dedicate their lives to it, must have its own positive program, distinct from all others. Reaffirming the basic principles of the first four congresses of the Comintern was not enough; the new International needed a program that would draw the necessary lessons from the cataclysmic events since those congresses, and answer the burning strategic and tactical problems facing the revolutionary movement in the 1930s. In fact, the organizational sides of the struggle for the Fourth International in the five-year period under examination were directly connected to, interlaced with, and dependent on the programmatic sides, the development of which fell mainly on Trotsky.

If I dwell on the organizational history rather than the programmatic contributions which were undoubtedly the main achievement of our movement in this period, it is only because the organizational side is less well known. A crucial advance in our analysis of the Soviet Union was made only a few weeks after the decision to work for a new International. Then, like now, we characterized the USSR as a degenerated workers' state, which revolutionaries must defend against imperialist attack. Until then, however, we had advocated not only reform of the Russian CP but also reform of the Soviet state. This, we decided late in 1933, was no longer realistic. The CP, we concluded, could not be reformed but would have to be opposed and replaced by a Soviet section of the Fourth International; and forcible action to oust the bureaucratic Stalinist caste from power (not just reform) was needed to restore workers' democracy in the Soviet state and society. Subsequently refined as the concept of the political revolution, this has been our bedrock position on the Soviet Union and degenerated and deformed workers' states ever since. Hardly anyone in the ICL disagreed with it when Trotsky formulated it in October 1933,[6] but differences about the class character of the USSR and what to do about it did begin to grow as the years went by and the crimes of Stalinism mounted. Our position was rejected by a third of the delegates to a national conference of the French section in 1937, and it was a major source of the important SWP split in 1940, where almost half the members were against defending the USSR when it came under imperialist attack in World War II.

Making a correct analysis of Stalinism as it evolved was only one of the important programmatic achievements that put their stamp on the Fourth International and conditioned its internal crises and conflicts in the thirties. Others related to our basic positions on fascism and the united front against it (Germany), People's Frontism (France and Spain), civil war (Spain), national liberation struggles against imperialism (China), and revolutionary policy in the fight against imperialist war. It would be hard to recognize the Fourth International without these programmatic positions. But they did not come easily or automatically. Reaching them required bitter struggle inside the movement as well as outside.

We now have come to the year 1934. In February, right wingers and fascists tried to overthrow the French bourgeois-democratic government; also in February, the Bonapartist government of Austria crushed an armed uprising by the Social Democratic workers; and in October, the Spanish right wing government crushed an armed uprising led by the Socialist Party. Trotsky considered the French developments to be the most crucial. France is now the key to the international situation, he wrote in a manifesto published in March; he had used the same terms to apply to Germany in the 1930-33 period. By this he meant that the center of revolutionary gravity in Europe had shifted to France; that a struggle decisive for the whole world had opened in that country; that a correct policy there could create the conditions for a revolutionary victory, with all the international repercussions that that would bring, and for a qualitative change in the growth of the movement for the Fourth International.

In keeping with his analysis of the potential situation in France, Trotsky threw himself and everything he had into trying to influence its development. He was hampered when the French press launched a big witch hunt against him in April and the government ordered him deported, because this meant he had to leave the metropolitan area where he had been able to attend IS meetings. Thereafter his direct participation was limited to what he could write or tell an occasional visitor to his home in a remote Alpine village. But his concern with the French section and its work never flagged.

The attempted French coup d'etat in February 1934 brought a militant response from the French workers, first a general strike and then overwhelming sentiment for a workers' united front against fascism. This was so strong that first the Socialist Party and then, more slowly, the Communist Party had to consent to a united front. Along with this grew talk and pressure for a merger of these two parties. At this point, in June 1934, Trotsky, who was on the run from one place to another and had not yet been granted permission to live in the French Alps, made an audacious proposal to the French section of the ICL: that it should formally dissolve and join the SP, which permitted tendencies inside the organization to exist and publish their own newspaper. This, he felt, would enable it to avoid isolation outside of the new united front and put it in a position to make recruits to its ideas among the large number of left-wing SP members who had joined or become radicalized since Hitler's victory.

Trotsky was the initiator of this entry tactic or maneuver, which came to be known as the "French turn." And he had to explain and defend this proposal with all the vigor and eloquence at his command[7] because it met much bigger resistance in the French section (and elsewhere) than the call for the new International had received. After a heated discussion and a near split averted only by IS intervention, the entry proposal was adopted by a majority of the French section at a national conference held at the end of August. It was supported by one of the two principal French leaders, Raymond Molinier, and opposed by the other, Pierre Naville. Shortly after the conference, the Naville group split from the section, and although it later decided to enter the SP too, it refused for a long time to join the Bolshevik-Leninist Group in the SP, which was the name now taken by the members of the French section.

The entry tactic was an affront and a blow to everyone in the ICL who was tainted by formalism, schematism, sectarianism, routinism, and passivity, and hid these traits behind radical rhetoric about revolutionary principles and Bolshevik firmness. These traits all came gushing out now. Some were opposed to the entry proposal on the ground that it was impermissible in principle under any circumstances; others were against it on tactical grounds, like Naville; and still others were opposed on any and all grounds.

It can be argued that entrism was only a tactic, and one which applied only in very specific circumstances. This is true enough, but in my opinion Trotsky's proposal was one of his finest contributions in the 1933-38 period. Aside from other benefits it

6. See "The Class Nature of the Soviet State" in *Writings of Leon Trotsky (1933-34)* (Pathfinder Press, New York, 1972).

7. Several articles on this subject are in *Writings of Leon Trotsky (1934-35)* (Pathfinder, 1971).

produced, the discussion it provoked shook up a lot of people and led to the first major liberation of our movement from the diseases of dogmatism that had been carried over from the Comintern or had been reinforced by different waves of recruits from third-period Stalinism. It also helped to rid us of people who were hopelessly unassimilable and could only hamper the healthy growth of our movement.

The repercussions in the IS and the ICL executive committee were bigger than those in the French section. Several members were opposed to the turn on various grounds, and most of them were incensed against Trotsky because he had taken the entry proposal to the French section before taking it up with the IS. Bauer, the IS secretary, denounced the proposal as a violation of Bolshevik principles and accused Trotsky of capitulating to the Second International. He could not even wait for the meeting of the ICL executive committee that was called for October to assess the French turn, but quit on the spot, and joined the German affiliate of the London Bureau. Sneevliet, the leader of the Dutch section, and Vereecken, the secretary of the Belgian section, were also opposed to the French turn, largely on tactical gounds, but Trotsky diplomatically persuaded them that even if they voted against the turn they should agree to let the French section, then already inside the SP, complete its experiment. The leadership of the Spanish section, long estranged from the ICL although still part of it, was vehemently against the French turn. The vote at the October meeting, which Trotsky could not attend, would have been even closer if Bauer had not quit so quickly and if the Spanish had not boycotted the meeting. As it was, Sneevliet, Vereecken and Pietro Tresso, a supporter of the Naville group, voted against the resolution written by Trotsky, which was adopted by a vote of 6 to 3.[8] One of the supporters of the resolution was Cannon of the American section, who had come at Trotsky's urging and was given the assignment of meeting with Bauer, Naville, and others and trying to persuade them they should not split the movement over a tactical question. Another of the supporters of the resolution was Molinier, who favored its main parts but objected so strongly to a provision in it inviting the Naville group to return to the French section that he threatened to resign from the executive committee. And it was at this time, Cannon later reported, that Sneevliet tried to convince him the whole ICL should join the London Bureau in order to take it over and into the Fourth International.[9]

Thus this 1934 dispute accounts for the departure of two more members of the 1933 group of eight leaders: Bauer and Naville (although Naville was to return before leaving for good in 1939). Bauer's defection to the London Bureau and Sneevliet's illusions about the London Bureau in 1934 also tell us something significant about the quality of their commitment to the Fourth International only a year after they became two of the four signers of the Declaration of Four.

Things began to pick up after the October meeting. The brightest spots were in France and the United States.

The American section had decided early in 1934 that the way to apply the new 1933 orientation in the U.S. was to propose a fusion with the left centrist American Workers Party, headed by A.J. Muste. (Contrary to the legends, this proposal originated with the American leaders, not with Trotsky, who approved it; and it was made before the Musteites wrote a glorious page of labor history in the Toledo Auto-Lite strike and before the American section showed its revolutionary caliber in the Minneapolis Teamster strikes.) There had been attempts in 1933 to fuse the German and Dutch sections with centrist groups in the London Bureau but they had fallen through. So the fusion of the American section with the AWP around a month after the October ICL meeting was the first time that this particular merger experiment was carried through. And it was a successful experiment, uniting the American cadre with an important group of effective mass workers and integrating most of them into the movement for the Fourth International.

One notable feature of the fusion was that the new Workers Party of the United States did not have any international affiliation at its birth. This was because the AWP had not had such affiliations and was not ready to adhere to the ICL. But this was only a temporary arrangement; seven months later virtually the whole leadership of the Workers Party voted to join with the ICL in working for the Fourth International. The success of the American fusion was contagious, at least in Holland, where the Dutch section and a centrist group headed by Peter Schmidt finally merged a few months later, early in 1935. This new Dutch party decided to belong to both the ICL and the London Bureau for the time being.

But the major advance took place in France, the key to the international situation. Within a few months, the Bolshevik-Leninist Group had tripled its membership and begun to influence thousands of left-wing Socialists; in the SP's youth organization they effected a bloc with the left-centrist leaders that soon had the reformist leaders worried. Even the die-hard sectarian Vereecken had to admit grudgingly that the Bolshevik-Leninists were doing good revolutionary work inside the French SP.

The Moscow bureaucracy finally began to junk its ultraleft third-period policies in the middle of 1934, when it gave permission to the French CP to form a united front with the SP. But neither Stalin, nor the French CP leaders, nor the French SP leaders, as it soon became clear, were interested in forming a united front of the workers against the capitalists. What they all wanted, for various reasons, was a front of the workers *with* some capitalists (bourgeois-democratic capitalists) against other capitalists (reactionary or fascist capitalists); that is, an alliance based on class collaboration instead of class struggle, which bore the name of People's Front when it came into existence. Stalin dropped the other shoe in May 1935 when he signed a nonaggression treaty with French imperialism and gave his blessings to French rearmament. What he was after was an alliance, in the name of "collective security," with peace-loving democratic imperialists (like France) against war-loving fascist imperialists (like Nazi Germany), and to get this alliance he was ready and eager to handcuff the French workers and deliver them into the custody of the French imperialists. That was the meaning of the People's Front that was organized by the bourgeois Radical Socialists, the Social Democrats and the Stalinists later in 1935.

All this put the French Bolshevik-Leninists in an extremely favorable position, precisely because they were inside the SP, to expose the real nature and aims of the People's Front and to rally the left wing workers to a revolutionary mobilization against the coming war. And this was also precisely why the SP leaders, egged on by the Stalinists, realized that they would have to expell the Fourth Internationalists from the SP and isolate them as much as possible as fast as possible.

Trotsky left France for Norway in June 1935, just as the SP leadership was preparing to move against the Bolshevik-Leninist Group. Sizing up the situation realistically, he advised his French comrades that their days in the SP were numbered and that they should orient quickly toward the construction of a new revolutionary party; for tactical reasons, they should take advantage of the democratic clauses in the SP's constitution to resist expulsions, expose the motives of the SP bureaucrats and solicit the sympathy of left wing workers, but all of this had to be subordinated to the political mobilization of an independent revolutionary party.

Trotsky also felt that the new social-patriotic policies of the Stalinists, which were universalized at the Seventh (and last)

8. See "The Present Situation in the Labor Movement and the Tasks of the Bolshevik-Leninists" in *Documents of the Fourth International: The Formative Years (1933-40)* (Pathfinder, 1973).

9. See Cannon's 1945 speech, "The Workers Party and the Minority in the SWP," in *The Struggle for Socialism in the "American Century"* (Pathfinder, 1977).

World Congress of the Comintern in 1935, and the worsening of the war danger, illustrated by fascist Italy's open preparations for the invasion of Ethiopia later in 1935, required an intensification of public work for the Fourth International, which had temporarily been subordinated to the exigencies of the French turn in France, Belgium, Poland, and elsewhere. So he wrote the text of a new document, the Open Letter for the Fourth International, which reaffirmed the 1933 Declaration of Four and brought it up to date in the light of the new developments since then. This was published in the summer of 1935.[10]

Unfortunately, an important part of the French leadership, headed by Molinier, did not agree with Trotsky's views on what to do in France, and the rest of the leadership, following Jean Rous and Naville, proved incapable of providing decisive action toward the construction of a new French party. Molinier thought the SP experience was not concluded and that additional gains could still be won in the SP. He felt this so strongly that he violated discipline and began publishing his own paper. The French section was plunged into the worst crisis in its history. Molinier's group was expelled at the end of 1935 and set up its own party. Precious time was lost. Many of the new recruits and sympathizers gained inside the SP were demoralized by the factionalism and drifted away. The two groups were reunited in June 1936, and then split again a few weeks later. It was a real mess, and accounted in part for the insignificant role the French section played during the big 1936 strike wave that followed the electoral victory of the People's Front, and the reduced role it played inside the Fourth International from then until World War II.[11]

In the heat of the dispute, which consumed much energy, Trotsky charged that the conduct of the Molinier group represented a capitulation to the social-patriotic pressures generated by the bourgeoisie in preparation for World War II and promoted by the Stalinists and Social Democrats. Then and later the Molinierists indignantly denied this charge, contending that the differences arose only over conflicting estimates as to how best to build a Fourth Internationalist party in France, and it is true that their subsequent evolution as an independent group did not have a social-patriotic character. But it seems equally true that if only tactical differences were involved, then splitting the French section at such a critical juncture was an irresponsible act that inflicted grave damage to the Fourth International in their own country and elsewhere, raising questions about the depth of their understanding about the need for the Fourth International as a united and disciplined movement. In any case, the splits resulted in the departure from the movement's leadership not only of Molinier but also of Pierre Frank, another of the group of eight in the 1933 international leadership. Frank did not return to the leadership until after World War II, during which the two French groups were finally reunited.

The French, Spanish and Belgian workers were radicalized in 1935 and 1936, but the radicalization was channeled into the People's Fronts, which came to power in France and Spain in 1936. People's Frontism became the central political issue, and the major obstacle to the growth of the Fourth International. Our movement produced a large body of propaganda and educational material on People's Frontism, but only a small vanguard was receptive to it at the time, although it represents political capital off which we are still living today. At the beginning nobody in the movement directly disputed the positions taken by Trotsky on People's Frontism, but again, as we shall see, it was a case for some members and leaders of abstract agreement at first, later followed by concrete serious divergences.

Before discussing the differences of People's Frontism, however, mention should be made of our international conference in July 1936. Although it was the only international conference we held between 1933 and the founding conference in 1938, and although it casts light on the state of the movement around the halfway point in our story, it is rarely discussed in our literature.

The Open Letter for the Fourth International in 1935 had proclaimed the need for its supporters to correlate and unify their work on a world scale under the banner of the Fourth International and held out the perspective of an international conference when conditions permitted. In 1936 the ICL decided the time had come for such a conference, and set it for April. But the conference was poorly prepared. Sneevliet and Peter Schmidt of the Dutch section were put in charge, but instead of organizing the conference, they ignored or obstructed it, and it had to be postponed from April to July. In the final weeks the Dutch leaders even let it be known that because of organizational grievances against the IS and Trotsky they did not intend to attend the conference. The main resolutions had to be written at the last minute, chiefly by Trotsky in Norway, so that there was no real preconference discussion. Trotsky also organized pressure on the Dutch section, so that Sneevliet finally had to attend. Altogether, only eight sections were represented[12]; others were invited but could not attend or did not receive invitations.

The July 1936 gathering was held a couple of months after the big French strike wave, two months after the American section publicly announced its members were entering the Socialist Party, around a week after the start of the Spanish civil war, and a few days after the second split in the French section.

Designating itself as the First International Conference for the Fourth International, this conference dissolved the ICL, established the Movement for the Fourth International (MFI), and expressed hope that a first constituent congress of the Fourth International could be held in seven or so months, after further discussion and the preparation of programmatic documents. The minutes of this conference were lost. For the last nine years we have been trying to get a complete picture of its proceedings, but most of the delegates are dead and most of the others either do not remember what happened or won't discuss it with us. The excellent political resolution on the new revolutionary upsurge in France and Spain and the other resolutions adopted—on the need for political revolution in the Soviet Union, on the London bureau, etc.—are all available and in print.[13] We also know about the structure chosen for the organization and its personnel: a General Council, equivalent to an international executive committee; an International Bureau of eleven; and an International Secretariat of five. But at least one aspect of the conference can now be clarified.[14]

The time has come to put to rest the principal legend about this conference, which I must admit with regret I have been helping to circulate for the last decade. I refer to the legend according to which Trotsky proposed that this conference should found or proclaim the foundation of the Fourth International and according to which the delegates to this conference rejected or refused to accept his proposal. How did this legend arise? There isn't the slightest basis for it in any of the surviving documents of the conference, or in the presently available correspondence about the conference in 1936 by Trotsky or anyone else.[15] None of the conference delegates interviewed in the last decade could recall any "proclamation" proposal by Trotsky at the conference or any action by the delegates to reject such a proposal. And some correspondence by delegates in 1936, which has become available to us only in the last year, thoroughly contradicts the legend.

10. See *Writings of Leon Trotsky (1935-36)* (Pathfinder, 1977).

11. See *The Crisis of the French Section (1935-36)* (Pathfinder, 1977).

12. France, Belgium, Holland, Britain, Germany, Italy, the USSR, and the United States.

13. See *Documents of the Fourth International.*

14. The following three paragraphs were rewritten in 1979 to correct erroneous statements made in the August 1978 talk.

15. A useful example of such correspondence is Max Shachtman's report to Trotsky two weeks after the conference, printed here as Appendix B (page 17).

So what is its source? Probably the statement Trotsky made two years later, in 1938, when he was arguing in favor of dropping the name "Movement for the Fourth International" and in favor of establishing the International at the international conference later that year: "This name [Movement for the Fourth International] seemed pedantic, unfitting, and slightly ridiculous to me even two years ago, when it was first adopted." But all that says is that Trotsky didn't like the name adopted; it doesn't at all follow from this statement that he made any proposal or that the delegates rejected it. Stretch that statement however you like, it cannot offer the slightest scrap of evidence for the alleged proposal and the alleged rejection.[16]

Discarding the legend and its implications about the delegates should not lead us to the opposite error of imagining that the conference was marked by nothing but harmony and agreement on perspectives. Sneevliet, who already was steering the Dutch section away from the Fourth International and toward the London Bureau, was the main adversary of the ICL leadership at the conference. He did not discuss his views on the International at the conference; in fact, he walked out of it because he did not like the order of the agenda. It is not likely that he would have gotten any significant support at this conference for his views on the International, and I think it is likely that most of the other delegates would have voted for a "proclamation" proposal if Trotsky had made one. But Sneevliet was not the only delegate in 1936 who left the movement before the founding conference in 1938; the Fourth Internationalist convictions of several other 1936 delegates crumbled or expired in the next two years. We will get fuller details in 1980, when Harvard will open the last of the Trotsky archives, but we already know that there were different concepts in the movement about the nature of the Fourth International, and different degrees of commitment to it, three years after it was first proposed.

Returning now to the problem of People's Frontism: Trotsky called attention to a dangerous tendency in the French section as early as October 1935, a few weeks after the People's Front was organized. Some members, he noted, were against raising a slogan calling for the Radical Socialists to be ousted from the People's Front; they thought that the workers "had to go through the experience" of having the People's Front in power, and therefore we had to support the People's Front as a whole. These comrades were not for People's Frontism themselves, of course not, but they held that we had to go along with the workers who were going along with the People's Front, and therefore. . . . The people holding such and similar views were a minority of the movement, but are worth remembering as evidence that even on questions as elementary as People's Frontism, our present positions did not come to us automatically but as the result of struggle against rather strong pressures. Sad to say, this position was not limited to new members recently won from the Socialist Party; it was also advanced by Ruth Fischer, the former German CP leader who was then a member of the IS and the ICL executive committee, who wanted our movement to call for power to the People's Front (including the bourgeois Radicals).

But the principal and most disruptive division over People's Frontism came around the Spanish POUM (Workers Party of Marxist Unification), its adaptation to the People's Front, and the defense of the POUM by important MFI sections and leaders. The POUM was formed in September 1935 as a merger between the centrist Workers and Peasants Bloc led by Joaquin Maurin and the Spanish section of the ICL, led by Andres Nin. The Spanish section had supported the call for a new International in 1933, but its disaffection with the IS and Trotsky soon led it to withdraw from all activities in the ICL while not formally disaffiliating from it. In 1934 it denounced the French turn and refused to join the Spanish SP even when the SP's youth group passed resolutions calling for a new International.

After the merger the POUM voted to affiliate to the London Bureau. But the ICL did not terminate relations with the POUM until January 1936, when the POUM, using the pretext that this was the only way it could get on the ballot in coming national elections, publicly endorsed the electoral program of the Spanish People's Front. Trotsky called this a betrayal of the workers, and after the Spanish civil war began in July, this characterization became the focus of a bitter debate in the MFI.

The POUM played a prominent role in driving back the fascists at the start of the civil war, and for a short time the ICL leaders hoped that in the crucible of war the POUM would correct its mistakes and that a reconciliation would take place. Trotsky also supported such an approach, volunteering to help by moving from Norway to Barcelona if possible. But in September Nin accepted the post of minister of justice in the Catalan People's Front government, and Trotsky resumed implacable criticism of the POUM, calling for the establishment of a Fourth Internationalist party in Spain after the POUM prohibited a pro-Fourth International tendency in its ranks. It took longer before other leaders and the principal sections of the MFI gave up their hopes that the POUM could be reformed, as a reading of their press late in 1936 shows. And some of the leaders never gave up their hopes and sympathy for the POUM.

The most outspoken defenders of the POUM in the MFI were Sneevliet, Vereecken, and Victor Serge, an Oppositionist who was allowed to leave the Soviet Union in 1936 and was elected to the MFI's General Council at the 1936 conference. They did not advocate People's Frontism and on occasion they even criticized the POUM's "mistakes" in this respect, but they denied that these mistakes were decisive and demanded that the MFI give complete political support to the POUM as the only revolutionary force in Spain. Their adaptation to People's Frontism took the form of pro-POUMism. This was the issue on which Serge broke from the MFI in 1937 after a meeting of the International Bureau rejected adaptation to the POUM. This was one of the issues on which the Dutch section separated itself from the MFI, although the actual formal break did not come until 1938. And it was the issue on which Vereecken fought a rearguard action against the IS throughout 1937, although he too did not resign until 1938.

Two weeks after the MFI conference, and even before its

16. The legend's earliest appearance in print that I have found was in Pierre Frank's short book, *La quatrieme internationale* (Francois Maspero, Paris, 1969); the 1972 English translation in *Intercontinental Press* was recently republished under the title *The Fourth International: The Long March of the Trotskyists* (Ink Links, London, 1979). It had only two sentences about the 1936 conference, one of which said: "Trotsky wanted the birth of the Fourth International announced then and there, but his proposal was not accepted by the conference, which called itself merely 'Movement for the Fourth International.'" Frank himself was not a delegate to the conference, nor did he attend it, so his statement was not based on eyewitness experience. Although he did not cite any documentary or other evidence, I accepted it as a factual statement, and repeated it in many books and other places, assuming that when he wrote on the subject with more room at his disposal he would fill in the information gaps. That occasion arrived at the end of 1978 when the first volume in a series called *Les congres de la quatrieme internationale* was published (Editions la Breche, Paris, 1978) with a substantial introduction by Frank that includes almost two pages about the 1936 conference. Alas, there are no more facts in these two pages than there were in his two 1969 sentences. The extra space is used by the author of the introduction for rhetoric and embroidery: "Why did he present this proposal? Why did the conference reject it? Why did the conference decide only to take the name of Movement for the Fourth International?," etc. But his answers, whether relevant or irrelevant, are locked so tightly between speculation and abstraction that mere facts cannot possibly wiggle their way in. Trotsky's May 31, 1938, letter, "'For' the Fourth International? No! The Fourth International!" is in *The Transitional Program for Socialist Revolution* (Pathfinder, 1977). His 1936 views on when and how to found the new International are in *Writings of Leon Trotsky (1935-36)* and *Supplement, Writings of Leon Trotsky,* and are discussed in Appendix C.

documents could be published anywhere, Stalin shocked the whole world by announcing the opening of the first big Moscow "confession" trial. Zinoviev and Kamenev were the chief defendants in the dock, but Trotsky and the Fourth International were the chief targets of this frame-up: its aim was to drive them out of the workers' movement throughout the world, to isolate them permanently as political pariahs whom no decent worker would talk to. Trotsky and the MFI had to, in effect, put everything else aside for almost a whole year in order to defend themselves in this life-or-death struggle. On the whole, they acquitted themselves well in exposing the frame-ups and their meaning. But little energy was left for other party-building and International-building activities in this period, and as a result the projected founding congress of the International had to be postponed.

The price of the Moscow trials went beyond that, however. The trials were a serious blow to the morale of revolutionary workers everywhere. Anti-Bolshevik tendencies appeared or were revived among workers previously sympathetic to the Russian revolution. Many activists, influenced by the joint bourgeois and Stalinist propaganda that Stalinism is the logical continuation of Leninism, became disillusioned with politics and withdrew to the sidelines. And the MFI was not immune to such defections and backsliding—neither its sympathizers, nor its members, nor its leaders.

It must seem strange to some that leading people who had been calling and working for the Fourth International should renounce and desert that work because of the crimes of Stalinism; after all, those crimes had been part of the reason they decided a new International was necessary. Yet that is precisely what happened with people like Muste and Schmidt, who had both been elected to the General Council at the 1936 conference. Barely a month after the conference and a few days after the first Moscow trial, they both resigned, Muste returning to pacifism and the church from which he had come originally, Schmidt returning soon after to the Social Democracy. Bourgeois pressures work in different ways on different people to destroy their belief in the capacity of the workers to liberate themselves from the oppressions of class society, and Stalinophobia, the fear and hatred of Stalinism to the exclusion of every other consideration, has been one of the most effective mechanisms for undermining and obliterating revolutionary consciousness during the last four decades.

We must remember that at the same time the Stalinists were murdering and imprisoning millions in the Soviet Union, they were winning millions of supporters in other countries by being the most active and ardent architects of alliances that they said would stop fascism and war. In 1939, of course, Stalin signed his pact with Hitler and that pact signaled the start of World War II, but in the preceding years many people were attracted to the Stalinists because they were the chief force calling for resistance to fascism and the coming war. Among these were not only newly politicized elements but political veterans like Alfonso Leonetti, a founder of the Italian CP, a founder of the Italian Left Opposition, and a member of the IS from 1930 to 1936 who was elected to the International Bureau at the 1936 conference. Leonetti had come to our movement during the Stalinist third-period and sectarian madness, and when the Stalinist line was switched he was as critical of People's Frontism as any other ICL leader.[17] But seeing no other mass alternative to war and fascism, he began gradually to see possible positive features in People's Frontism, and soon after the 1936 conference he became inactive and then dropped away. The pressures operating on him became more evident during the war, when he collaborated with the Stalinists in France; and after the war he applied for readmission into the Italian CP, where he was accepted and is now a "Eurocommunist."

17. Leonetti's articles on this subject in the ICL press used the pseudonyms J.P. Martin and A. Feroci.

Leonetti was the last of the eight leaders we singled out for 1933. To repeat: Three were murdered by the GPU (Trotsky, Sedov, and Klement); and one capitulated to the Stalinists (Leonetti). Two split away from the movement temporarily because of tactical differences (Frank and Naville, Naville later leaving permanently because of deeper differences). And two split away to join the centrist London Bureau (Bauer of the German section and Sneevliet with the Dutch section). Bauer was a sectarian formalist while Sneevliet adapted himself to POUMist opportunism but they both ended up in the same centrist pit, and Naville would have joined them if the London Bureau had not gone out of business before he got there. Leonetti's adaptation to People's Frontism led him to Stalinism while Sneevliet's adaptation to the POUM's participation in the People's Front led him to the London Bureau, but in both cases it led away from the Fourth International. Anyone who thinks the ICL and the MFI were immune to People's Front pressures has to overlook such evidence about what was impeding the Fourth International internally. Our list of defectors could be extended, but the losses among the eight are sufficient to show what a variety of pressures beat down on these people, with a force that drove some of them far from the goal of the Fourth International that they had set themselves only a couple of years before.

In Mexico Trotsky completed the major part of his historic exposure of the Moscow trials in mid-1937. Then he turned again to the internal problems of the movement, and he reached agreement with the IS on the need for another and better prepared international conference, tentatively slated for October 1937. But it had to be postponed, partly because the American section had been expelled from the SP and needed time for adequate preparation of the convention that established the SWP at the end of the year.

In March 1938 an SWP delegation, consisting of Cannon, Shachtman, V.R. Dunne and Rose Karsner, visited Trotsky in Mexico to discuss the proposed international conference. Transcripts of the major discussions, which also involved several important American problems, will be found in the books *The Transitional Program for Socialist Revolution* and *Trotsky's Writings 1937-38*. They are worth reading, or rereading, on the occasion of this fortieth anniversary because they provide an excellent example of Trotsky's method of collaborating with other leaders of the movement. First of all, he did not just talk to them or at them—he also listened very carefully, and he learned as well as taught. Benefits of this approach are to be seen in the main programmatic document he wrote for the founding conference, but they extended far beyond the most important document. Because the method Trotsky used promoted the spirit of teamwork, which is indispensable for the creation of a collective leadership.

In the first of the discussions in Mexico agreement was reached on the nature and timing of the international conference, on the documents that had to be prepared, especially a programmatic series of transitional demands, and so on. Then Cannon said:

"On the organizational side of the question—shall we consider this conference as a provisional gathering or as the actual founding of the Fourth International? The prevailing opinion among us is that we would actually form the Fourth International at this conference. We think that the main elements of the Fourth International are now crystallized. We should put an end to our negotiations and maneuvers with the centrists and henceforth deal with them as separate and alien groupings."

Trotsky replied that he agreed "absolutely" with what Cannon said. And for the benefit of the SWP leaders who would be attending the international conference he listed the forces in the MFI that would or might be opposed to such a concept of the international conference: some of the Belgians, especially Vereecken; some of the French; Sneevliet and a majority of the Dutch. "Naturally we are a weak International," he said, "but we are an International." He urged the Americans to push their position energetically.

Cannon then continued: "Some comrades have taken the tactic of maneuvering and making concessions to centrists as a permanent policy, whereas we think that all our maneuvers with the centrists have been exhausted by now. We were justified two, three, or four years ago in delaying organizational action, in order to complete the maneuvers and experiments with those people, but not now. We noticed in our discussions that there are some comrades who want to carry over the tactic indefinitely—some kinds of maneuvers which are doomed in advance to defeat. And for this reason I believe we have to explain this matter to the comrades."

Trotsky said he subscribed to every word of Cannon's along these lines. The exchange is significant only because it would not have taken place, and would not have been necessary, if the views it expressed were shared by everyone in the MFI. And remember, this was only five months before the founding conference.

In May Trotsky submitted a very emphatic letter to a Czech comrade as a contribution to the international preconference discussion. It was entitled, "'For' the Fourth International? No! The Fourth International!" On reading this letter Vereecken resigned from the movement. Sneevliet and the Dutch section had already departed. There was some French opposition to founding the new International but it was a minority view. At the conference itself nineteen of the delegates voted in favor of a statute proclaiming the founding of the International, while three voted against: the two delegates from the Polish section and Yvan Craipeau of the French section.[18]

The Polish delegates in 1938 were not opposed to founding the International, they said, but they were opposed to doing it at this time, because it would be a meaningless gesture, because we were too small, and because the first three Internationals had all been founded in periods of revolutionary upsurge.[19] The three opponents of the founding did not specify how deep a revolutionary upsurge would have to be before they would agree to a new International, but in any case they did not wait around too long. One of the Poles became a Zionist, the other dropped out of politics, and Craipeau quit after the war to join a series of centrist outfits who were all opponents of the Fourth International. The supporters of the founding generally agreed with Trotsky's view that the existing national sections needed a clearly defined international organization and leadership, whatever its size might be.

It is tempting to speculate how the vote would have gone if Trotsky and the SWP had not taken such a strong stand. By the end of the war and the political holocaust it visited on the revolutionary movement, five of the fifteen International Executive Committee members elected at the founding conference had been killed, and of the remaining ten only two were still active in our movement: Cannon and Carl Skoglund of Minneapolis.

The other great achievement of 1938 was the transitional program, which Trotsky wrote and asked the SWP to sponsor in the international discussion. It is unquestionably the most valuable programmatic document produced by the revolutionary movement since Lenin's time. It draws upon the actual experiences of the workers internationally in the epoch of imperialism, summarizes and synthesizes the lessons of their struggles, and projects a program and a method for leading the workers and their allies at their current levels of consciousness across the bridge to the struggle for workers' power. Despite different conditions, the transitional method is as relevant and usable today as it was forty years ago. The transitional program put an indelible stamp on our movement—the Fourth International and the SWP would be quite different and much weaker without it. I am not sure that they would have survived the crippling adversities of the forties and fifties without such a program and method.

That completes our narrative, but leaves us with a couple of questions to consider. One of these, almost poking us in the eye, is whether the Fourth International would have been founded at all in 1938 without Trotsky. His role was so overwhelming that our critics at that time derided it as a one-man International, certain to disintegrate and fall apart as soon as Trotsky was gone. This prediction was soon put to a test when Trotsky was murdered in 1940, and it was refuted in the maelstrom of World War II, when the International was badly maimed and mauled but succeeded nevertheless in holding fast to its principles and remaining the authentic continuator of revolutionary internationalism. As Cannon said at a 1940 memorial meeting, Trotsky had built this movement around ideas, not personalities, and the ideas survived after his death.

The question we are raising is very much like the one that is asked about Lenin: if, early in 1917, a brick had fallen off a roof in Zurich where Lenin was in exile and had fallen on Lenin and killed him, would the October revolution have taken place in Russia later that year? Most of the people who pose that question think it is very cute: if you say Yes, the revolution would have taken place without Lenin, that proves you are blind to the facts and dogmatically denying the importance of the role of the individual in history. If you say No, the revolution would not have taken place without Lenin, then you are convicted, in their eyes, of violating the doctrines of historical materialism, underestimating class forces and the role of the masses, and giving an exaggerated, unwarranted, and idealistic significance to the role of great individuals or heroes in history.

But leaving games aside, Marxists don't have to make concessions to anybody when they examine the concrete developments in 1917 and conclude that without Lenin the October revolution in all probability would not have taken place when it did or would not have been successful if attempted. Genuine Marxism finds no contradiction between the role of the revolutionary masses and the role of exceptional, even indispensable revolutionary leaders; both are needed for success. It is true that in the early years of this century, when much of the movement was still in its theoretical adolescence, some of its leaders propounded a version of Marxism that was steeped in fatalism, in a vision of socialism arriving through the inevitable advance of impersonal economic forces and ignoring or underestimating the crucial role of leadership. But since 1917 and the assimilation of Bolshevism as the revolutionary essence of Marxism in the epoch of imperialism, these errors have been corrected among authentic Marxists, who reject fatalism, understand the limits and pitfalls of spontaneism, and accord a more correct weight to the indispensability of leadership in theory and in practice, especially collective leadership.

In a 1935 discussion about underground activity in Nazi Germany, Trotsky warned the German comrades against what he thought was a tendency to take a supercilious or contemptuous attitude toward those members of our underground movement who were not well educated in Marxist literature and theory. I can't describe the whole discussion here, but I want to cite one passage from Trotsky that I think is pertinent:

"Moreover, one makes the revolution with relatively few Marx-

18. See "Minutes of the Founding Conference of the Fourth International" in *Documents of the Fourth International*. Eleven sections were represented by regular delegates at this conference: the United States, France, Britain, Germany, the USSR, Italy, Brazil, Poland, Belgium, Holland, and Greece. Several other sections expressed their adherence to the new International even though they were unable to send delegates. There is no evidence that the Fourth International as a whole had any more members at the time of its founding conference than the International Left Opposition had in 1933.

19. In the United States around this time Walter Reuther was starting to explain that he was not opposed to the founding of a labor party, "but now is not the time."

ists, even within the party. Here the collective substitutes for what the individual cannot achieve. The individual can hardly master each separate area—it is necessary to have specialists who supplement one another. Such specialists are often quite passable 'Marxists' without being complete Marxists, because they work under the supervision of genuine Marxists. The whole Bolshevik Party is a marvelous example of this. Under Lenin's and Trotsky's supervision, Bukharin, Molotov, Tomsky, and a hundred others were good Marxists, capable of great accomplishments. As soon as this supervision was gone, even they collapsed disgracefully. This was not because Marxism is a secret science, it is just very difficult to escape the colossal pressures of the bourgeois environment with all of its influences."[20]

It would be totally misleading to read this passage as meaning that Trotsky was indifferent to the education and training of Marxist cadres; his whole life was dedicated to developing them. What he is actually saying, in my opinion, is that while we are engaged in training Marxist cadres, we must not set ourselves impossible or ideal standards but must recognize that as long as the bourgeois environment continues to press down upon all of us, not everyone is going to turn out to be a "complete" or perfect Marxist. We must use the forces available, even with their defects, attempting to strengthen, guide and supervise them so that they make the most effective contributions to our common revolutionary work. In addition, it seems to me , Trotsky is making the bigger point that while there are few "complete Marxists" *their* role is of decisive importance because on what they do or do not do depends the success or failure of all the others, the less-than-complete Marxists, and therefore of the movement as a whole. Far from belittling the role of Marxist leadership, Trotsky here was attributing to it, in a very concrete way, a centrality and decisiveness such as I have not found expressed elsewhere in his or Lenin's writings. It is not an elitist conception at all, but an understanding of the unprecedented leadership responsibilities that the most competent Marxists bear. And this understanding permeated everything he thought and did about the Fourth International.

When Trotsky wrote in his diary in 1935 that he thought the building of the Fourth International was the most important work he had ever done, commentators like Isaac Deutscher found it impossible to believe that a person of Trotsky's intelligence meant or could mean this literally. But Trotsky did mean it literally, and he acted accordingly, with every resource at his disposal.

We all knew that Trotsky was the theoretical leader of the movement; every one of our many conquests in this area in the thirties originated with him or bore his imprint. But we did not all know, until the recent publication of the *Writings* series, how much Trotsky was also the practical-political leader of the International. The circumstances of his exile did not permit him to attend our international conferences and he was able to participate in the meetings of the IS for only a few months while he lived in France. But despite all the legal restrictions and the obstacles of time and space, he succeeded in various ways in placing himself politically at the center of the leadership and of participating in all the major decisions, not only the strategic ones but very often the tactical ones too. His role in the active leadership of the Fourth International and its predecessors was bigger and lasted longer than that of Marx and Engels in the First International, Engels in the Second, and Lenin in the Third.

I also suspect that few of us have adequately appreciated how much the fate of the Fourth International in those years depended on the will of a single person. (I use the words will, will power, or determination to reach your goal where Trotsky's critics would say "fanaticism" or "dogmatic stubbornness" or "doctrinal blindness to reality" or something like that.) Fortunately for the movement, Trotsky possessed this element in great abundance—enough to keep him going against great odds, with enough left over to provide the stimulus for others whom he drew along, perhaps dragged along, beyond their normal capacities while he was alive, after which some of them wilted and dropped away.

I didn't think I had to persuade this audience that revolutionary workers need to be organized internationally as well as nationally or that the founding of the Fourth International was necessary and progressive. But there is a corollary question that may need clarification here: Granted that the International had to be founded, why was its founding in 1938 so urgent, what difference would it have made if it had not been founded until later?

The main answer is World War II. It almost broke out in the Munich crisis the same month the conference was held, and it did actually begin just one year later. Next to revolution, war is the supreme test for revolutionary organizations. It submits them to overwhelming pressures, it often isolates them or isolates them further from their base, it strips them of illusions, it crushes the weak and wavering elements, it poses life-or-death challenges to the strong. Within weeks or months, World War II swept away the London Bureau and the remnants of the Brandlerite international like gnats in a hurricane.

The small and weak Fourth International was not immune to these destructive and disintegrative influences. On the European continent, the national sections were driven underground and reduced to a handful by ruthless repression. Some members of the 1938 International Executive Committee were murdered at their posts: Trotsky by a GPU agent in Mexico, Leon Lesoil by the Nazis in a concentration camp, Pietro Tresso by the Stalinists in France, Ta Tu Thau by the Stalinists in Vietnam. Others withdrew to the sidelines or defected. Pioneers like Shachtman, even before the United States entered the war, buckled under the weight of bourgeois-democratic opinion, rebelled against the perspectives of the Fourth International they had voted for at the founding conference, and led a damaging split of the movement. Slowly, our heroic comrades were able to reknit some of the European sections and resume activity against their formidable enemies, but they took over four years of the war before they succeeded in reestablishing connections among themselves in the form of a European secretariat of the Fourth International.

So it is safe to say that if the International had not been founded in 1938, it would not have been founded during the war. Eventually, sooner or later, it would have been founded, but it would have been a different and politically weaker body than the one that was established in 1938 and managed to survive the war with its banner and tradition unstained.

During the war itself, the existence of the International—cribbed, cabined and confined as it was when the center was moved to the United States—was an enormous factor in maintaining revolutionary morale and ideological continuity in the midst of adversity. I can report personally how much it strengthened me as a youthful activist to know that the International and its partisans, even though cut off from each other, were continuing the struggle for our common ideas and goals. Later in the war, after I had been drafted into the army and sent to France, where political conditions were much more difficult than here, I had a chance to talk with many European comrades, and to hear over and over again testimony about the unifying and inspirational effects that news (or even just rumors) about the existence and survival of the Fourth International had on the persecuted fighters in the concentration camps, prisons, armies and underground cells. They fought better because of this, and it would have been harder for them to keep on fighting without it. And without it, it would have been more difficult to establish the political and ideological homogeneity that was established soon after the war.

Hard as it was to found the International in 1938, with Trotsky's help, it would have been harder to found it after the war,

20. See "Underground Work in Nazi Germany," a transcript of a discussion held around June 1935, in *Supplement, Writings of Leon Trotsky*.

when the authority of the would-be founders would have been smaller and the precious continuity of the movement would have been sundered for several years. Not only would it have been harder to found it after the war, but it also would have been harder to maintain its unity after it was founded. Keeping the International together in the face of external pressures and internal disputes has never been easy, and sometimes it has not been possible, but it would have been much more difficult if the efforts to found it in 1938 had ended in failure.

The Fourth International, like the parties affiliated or sympathetic to it, is not yet strong or influential enough anywhere to complete the mission it undertook in 1938. But it is many times larger than it was then, larger than it has ever been, and still growing. It does not have a Trotsky to guide it, but it has a collective leadership, which it lacked in Trotsky's time. It still has to cope with many serious problems, but none are the fatal sort that wrecked the First, Second and Third Internationals. It has lived longer than any of these predecessors, but it is still young, vigorous, able to learn and correct mistakes, and revolutionary in its outlook and practice. It embodies the revolutionary lessons, traditions, methods, and program of the past century and a third, and the destiny of humanity depends on its future. In large part this is due to the way it was conceived and nurtured in the five years we have examined.

Appendix A
The International Opposition and the Communist International[1]

The events that have unfolded in Germany and have resulted in the establishment of fascism and the bankruptcy of the German Communist Party have posed the question before the International Left Opposition of a new party in Germany, a question that has been broadly discussed in our ranks and has been definitively settled.[2]

On the basis of the German events the May plenum unanimously adopted the orientation toward the construction of a genuinely communist party in Germany. Before this plenum, since the betrayal in Germany committed by the Stalinist party, voices were raised in our ranks calling for a new international orientation. "How can we condemn the German party without at the same time condemning the Communist International, which led the party and bears the real responsibility for this betrayal?" was the usual way the comrades argued. The events in Austria and Bulgaria,[3] proving that neither the International nor the parties were capable of learning the slightest lesson from the German catastrophe, but instead actively sought to justify the ill-fated policy followed in Germany, and even characterized the present situation as a victory—these events have broadened our criticism toward those who are really responsible for the German betrayal, and have forced us to pose the question of our attitude towards the International, and to settle it in a clear and definitive manner.

Should we continue to consider ourselves as a faction of the Comintern, or break definitively from it and disassociate ourselves from responsibility for the policies of the faction that leads the International? Should we persevere in our orientation toward reform, or put an end to it, and orient towards a new, independent regrouping of revolutionary forces on a world scale?

The International Secretariat has already explained to the sections in its circular how the question has been posed. Even though the discussion is only just beginning in the sections, it seems that the proposal for the new orientation has been favorably received. It is necessary that this historically important turn be preceded by a full discussion in order to clarify as fully as possible all the questions related to it and to sift out the tasks that flow from it.

It is now time to draw the balance sheet on what our position as a faction in the Comintern has given us, and to establish our position in the light of the experience gained from the German catastrophe up to the present day. The Comintern's abandonment of the line of its first congresses has come about in stages—most notable, the policy of the Anglo-Russian Committee, the defeat of the Chinese revolution, the gradual degeneration of the Russian Communist Party, and the treacherous capitulation before German fascism.[4]

This process of degeneration finds its expression in the international communist movement in the form of an ideological and organizational weakening of the parties. Although this whole

1. This was a resolution adopted by the executive committee of the International Left Opposition at a meeting ("plenum") in Paris on August 19, 1933. It was the first official document of the ILO calling for a new International. Although it is in accord with Trotsky's position at the time, it is not written in his style and appears to have been drafted by a non-French member of the IS after a discussion with Trotsky. It is translated here by Jeff White from the French text reprinted in *Naissance de la IVe Internationale (1933-1940)*, La Breche, Paris, 1978.

2. The proposal that the German section of the ILO should stop working for the reform of the German CP and start working for the creation of a new revolutionary party in Germany was debated in the ILO from March 1933, when Trotsky first made this proposal, until May 1933, when the ILO leadership approved it at a plenum in Paris. The leadership of the German section was opposed to the proposal at first, but by May they had changed their minds and supported the new orientation for Germany. Trotsky's letters and articles on this question are in *Writings 32-33* and *Supplement 29-33*. The May plenum resolution, entitled "On the Need for a New German Party," is in *Documents of the Fourth International.*

3. In the months following Hitler's victory in 1933, the Stalinists in Austria, Bulgaria, and elsewhere continued to oppose united front action against the fascists, as they had done in Germany. This led in Austria to the total suppression of the CP and in Bulgaria to the virtual suppression of the CP, in both cases with little or no protest from the workers.

4. The Anglo-Russian Trade Unity Committee existed from 1925 to 1927 as a bloc of "left" bureaucrats in the British Trades Union Congress with the Stalinist leadership of the Soviet unions. The Left Opposition demanded that the Soviet representatives break up the bloc after the British representatives had betrayed the 1926 general strike in Britain. The Stalinists clung to the bloc, claiming all kinds of revolutionary virtues for it until the British dissolved the committee by withdrawing in 1927. Trotsky's writings on the subject are in *Leon Trotsky on Britain.* The Chinese revolution of 1925-27 was crushed because the Chinese CP, following the orders of Stalin and Bukharin, subordinated the interests of the revolution to their alliance with the bourgeois nationalist forces headed by Chiang Kai-shek. For Trotsky's position, see *Leon Trotsky on China.* The gradual degeneration of the Russian CP began while Lenin was still alive. See *Lenin's Fight Against Stalinism* for articles sounding the alarm against Stalinism written by Lenin and Trotsky in 1922 and 1923, when they planned a joint attack on bureaucratism in the CPSU and the Soviet state.

degeneration has been determined principally by the establishment of the reactionary theory of "socialism in one country," it has nevertheless come about in stages, between which can be seen degrees of decomposition.

Our position as a faction has been determined by the reality out of which we came and in which we have been obliged to work. The proletarian character of the Soviet state and the existence of a party having the greatest traditions and of an international organization encompassing important revolutionary forces, constituted the forces on which we had to rely for an entire period for the possibility of the reform that we advocated. We had to exhaust all the possibilities that flowed from that reality before we could pose the question of a new orientation. It was an indispensable stage in those concrete conditions, an inevitable experience we had to undergo, and on the basis of which we had to work out our position at a certain decisive stage.

Is reform possible after the German experience and particularly after the lessons of these last months? And if it is no longer possible, what purpose is served by being a faction? Should we wait, fatalistically, for the same experience to repeat itself in every country, or for a catastrophe in Soviet Russia before abandoning our position as a faction? Or should we instead, as vanguard of the revolutionary movement, henceforth reject all responsibilities [for the Comintern], face up to reality, and enter on the road to the independent regroupment of the revolutionary forces on an international scale to wage the most bitter and effective struggle against world capitalism, and thereby give real support to the proletarian state?

Those are the questions we must answer. The force of the facts imposes a new orientation on us. This means that from now on we must look for every opportunity for unity and collaboration with the revolutionary forces who, since the German catastrophe, are beginning to break away from the influence of the Communist International led by the Stalinists, and from the Second International, and to orient themselves towards a communist movement founded on the principles formulated by the first congresses of the Comintern and on the experience acquired in the communist movement since the death of Lenin. This means that while rejecting responsibility for the Stalinists we must collaborate with the Stalinist organizations on the international, national, and local levels on the basis of the tactic of the united front, through which we must link up with and win over the best elements that still remain in the Stalinist parties. Even at the present stage of decay of the Comintern, the winning of these elements will constitute an important objective of our activity.

The lessons of the latest events after the German catastrophe have made our change of viewpoint on the international scale appear altogether logical. These lessons have also untied us from our attitude toward the Stalinist party in the Soviet Union.

The question of our attitude toward the CP of the USSR must be considered in conjunction with that of our attitude to the Communist International. On the one hand, our independent activity in the capitalist countries by the regroupment of revolutionary forces on the basis of authentic communist principles will forge the most effective weapon for the defense of the proletarian state; on the other hand, our bold attitude inside the Soviet Union will throw into greater relief the state of decay of the Stalinist party, arouse the attention of all the elements dedicated to the communist cause, show them the grievous danger that threatens the proletarian state, and give them a flag for struggling against reaction and sweeping aside the power of the centrist bureaucracy.

While adopting this new orientation in its general lines, the plenum underscores the heavy tasks that fall on our international organization in the coming period. More than ever the necessity is being brought home with particular force for strict cohesion in our ranks, for absolute clarity in our positions and principles, and for spreading our activity into all areas of action among the workers and oppressed layers.

These premises will allow us to apply a flexible tactic toward the currents that are oriented to communism and, on the basis of firm principles, to facilitate their assimilation of these principles and their definitive passage into the common camp of intransigent and merciless struggle for the overthrow of capitalism.

How are we to set up this new International?

By rooting our own forces in the ranks of the workers.

1. Consider ourselves as the embryo of the genuine communist party; establish in every section our program of very broad action; turn our backs resolutely on the work of reform and its particular characteristics; maintain fractions in all the labor organizations and handle our tactics in accordance with the relationship of forces.

Direct our fire mainly against the influence of the Social Democracy; be the propagandists and popularizers of communism and internationalism; strive to tear away the workers attached to the party by real action against the bourgeoisie and its lackeys. To that end, push the united front in action with the official CP at all levels. If the bureaucracy refuses, support the actions of the Stalinist parties if they are appropriate; oppose them if they are wrong.

2. With regard to the auxiliary organizations, International Red Aid,[5] etc., draw the conclusions from our new orientation. Wherever the International Red Aid shows it is only a tool of bureaucratic conservatism and of a tendency, create real organizations of revolutionary solidarity, according to our forces. What has been said on this subject is true for all the other auxiliary organizations of the party.

3. Declare that our previous analysis of the Soviet state as a workers' state with a pronounced bureaucratic degeneration is still our analysis, that the accentuation of the bureaucratic degeneration in the CPSU and the Comintern involves a decisive danger for the workers' state, and that the reconstitution of a party in the USSR and the strengthening of the revolutionary proletariat in the world around a revolutionary International are decisive factors in the defense of the workers' state.

Rally the revolutionary forces in the world by denouncing the inability of the Stalinist parties to defend the USSR. Struggle in the USSR for the reform of the state, the complete reestablishment of the prerogatives of the proletariat, and the defeat of the bureaucracy. Support at all times the proletarian forces against the Thermidorean forces—this will be the role of our section in the USSR, whose indispensable creation as the incarnation of communist and revolutionary principles will be the greatest assurance of the existence of the October revolution. In no way does it follow from this demand that we are disposed to accept the creation of other parties in the USSR. On this point the Left Opposition has changed nothing in its demands for workers' democracy as the pivot of the dictatorship of the proletariat.[6]

4. Our present forces, acting as an embryo of a communist party can, by their political cohesion, their testing in action among the working class organizations, and their resulting experience, exert an important attraction on other currents in the labor movement who have been repelled by the Third and Second Internationals, and who are moving towards communist positions. Our attractive power will be all the more pronounced when our position as a

5. The International Red Aid was organized in 1922 as a Comintern auxiliary organization to defend class struggle victims; under Stalinist control in the 1930s it discriminated against and refused to support the cases of Left Oppositionists arrested by the capitalists. In the United States its affiliate was called the International Labor Defense (ILD), which was organized in 1925.

6. As this passage indicates, the Left Opposition, while fighting for the restoration of workers' democracy and the reconstitution of a revolutionary party in the USSR, was still unwilling at this time in 1933 to advocate a multiparty system of pro-soviet parties in that country. It was not until 1938 that the Fourth International, in the transitional program, adopted the demand for the legalization of soviet parties in the USSR.

faction no longer exists as an obstacle between these currents and ourselves.

These are diverse formations; some are close to our position, others are still heterogeneous and require a great deal of work to assimilate to our positions. We must fight forcefully against the conception of an unprincipled grouping. On the contrary, the International Left Opposition must orient its forces to rally these scattered currents on the basis of communist principles.

It would not be a question of a regroupment between the Third and Second Internationals, but rather one based on the foundations of the Third International, which have been abandoned by the Comintern (the first four congresses in their main lines, enriched by the experience of the last ten years), and on the eleven points of the ILO preconference.[7]

5. Having defined the basis of political relations with the existing groups, the Left Opposition must understand the historical interest represented by the international regroupment of these scattered groups, who, without a foundation of well-defined principles and without organic ties, can degenerate in the present chaos or fall prey to the exterminative maneuvers of the Stalinists.

On the other hand the ILO must also understand that the disintegration of the Second and Third International will again give birth to further divisions and splits, and that in our relations with the groups that are moving towards communism we must demonstrate educational flexibility as well as political intransigence.

7. This refers to the platform adopted by the ILO preconference in February 1933. One of the eleven points, still calling for the policy of reform in the USSR, was later changed to recognize the need for a new International and new national parties.

Appendix B
A Report on the 1936 Conference[1]

Bronx, New York
August 13 [1936]

Dear Comrade Trotsky:

My last days in Paris were so occupied with the details of finishing off rag-ends of the postconference work and with the difficult business of obtaining passage back to New York during the tourist season that it is only now that I am able to write you some of my impressions.

On the whole, I would say that the conference accomplished everything that was to be expected of it and everything that we originally planned in Weksal. With one or two minor exceptions, we were able to deal with every point on the order of the day and to adopt motions or resolutions covering the most important problems, both political and organizational, which were posed before the conference. When you consider that we had only three days at our disposal, that we have no large technical apparatus at our command, and that we had a large agenda, I think that our modest accomplishments were something of an achievement. To the difficulties should of course be added the attitude of the Dutch delegate[2] which didn't improve the general efficiency of the conference.

We did not adopt a *special* resolution on France and Spain because the comrades assigned (Fero and Rous) [Alfonso Leonetti and Jean Rous] did not have the opportunity to finish it. Their draft was to be left to the incoming IS to edit and make public; in any case, the general resolution on the revolutionary upsurge covers the ground pretty well, and the lack of a special resolution is not fatal. Nor did we adopt the trade union thesis which came before the conference at the very last minute and only in a German translation; we were therefore compelled to refrain from considering it and decided instead to use it as the opening of an international discussion on the trade union question. Finally, I was unable to find the time for the communique to the bourgeois press and the draft is to be turned over the Naville to elaborate, in view of his connections with various journalists who are in a better position to get us some "publicity." As I remember it, these are the principal shortcomings of the conference, and all things considered, we did not do so badly. After the conference, we met in two or three long sessions of the new IS during which the adopted resolutions and amendments were finally edited so that nothing stands in the way of their publication immediately (at least in French, to begin with) except the purely technical work of typing the stencils and running them off on the machine.

The most important "internal" question before the conference was of course that of the Dutch party. Sneevliet's conduct was something unprecedented. The same [Dutch] party leadership which conducts itself so gracefully and un-ultimatistically in the London Bureau conferences—presumably conferences of our enemies and theirs—could find no other way of conducting itself at

1. By permission of the Library of Social History, New York. Max Shachtman was one of Trotsky's principal collaborators in planning and carrying throught the 1936 international conference. He knew better than anyone else exactly what Trotsky expected and hoped for from the conference. Shachtman and A.J. Muste were the delegates of the American section, which had recently joined the Socialist Party. Shachtman went to Europe early; he collaborated with the IS in Paris, he spent time in Amsterdam putting pressure on the Dutch section to attend the conference, and he visited Trotsky in Weksal, Norway, to explain what the IS intended to do at the conference and to get last-minute suggestions on tactics from Trotsky. This letter was written two weeks after the conference, when Shachtman had just got back to the U.S. It is a report about "internal" questions which Shachtman and Trotsky had discussed in considerable detail before the conference. Some of these problems were grave ones, others were minor and transitory. It is psychologically and politically impossible to believe that Shachtman would have troubled to report their outcome while at the same time failing to even mention Trotsky's alleged proposal for the conference to proclaim the Fourth International and the conference's alleged refusal to accept this proposal.

2. Henricus Sneevliet was the Dutch delegate. See the *Supplement* and *Writings of Leon Trotsky (1935-36)* for several letters about the role of the Dutch leadership up to the conference.

our conference than by manifesting supreme contempt for it and by facing it with ultimatums at every turn. Adolph [Rudolf Klement] has told me that he has already written you the details and I shall not therefore dwell upon them here. Sneevliet insouciantly came late to the conference; he stayed for an hour or two; he came that evening to the organization commission with a new ultimatum on the IS to be elected, in which he proposed to exclude all those who have had the misfortune to be defeated by Stalinism or fascism (i.e., the "emigre" sections, or as he calls them: the "abnormal" or "dead" sections); the next morning we receive a new ultimatum, threatening withdrawal, to which we reply in the most restrained and polite manner, despite our mounting indignation; the [Dutch] party bureau in Amsterdam, *by telephone*, directs Sneevliet to break with the conference, without troubling to hear our point of view—and Sneevliet, without another word, departs. (I recall, at this point, the outraged feelings of the Dutchmen when you sent us a telegram expressing your personal opinion about the "American turn," after having read both sides—a telegram which did not commit the American section; the Dutch, by telephone, on the basis of a one-sided report, *decide in two minutes* to break with the conference of the Fourth International, and in such a way that it can only be followed by further steps away from our whole movement and its political line. Apparently, these are the "organizational methods" that we are asked to substitute for "ours"!!!) As you know, we decided to write a letter to the CC [central committee] of the RSAP [Dutch section] concerning the whole affair; I drafted the text and sent it to the IS for approval and mailing. I hope that you find it a fitting reply both in tone and in content. As I see the aim of this letter, it is to set down, in friendly and nonpolemical manner, the *facts*, first of all, relating to the convening and carrying through of the conference; secondly, the impermissible conduct of Sneevliet at the conference (en passant, he did not even leave us the colonial thesis which he said he had brought along!); thirdly, the *enumeration*, without yet taking explicit position, of the undoubted *political* differences that exist between us; fourth, an attempt at a popular explanation, so simple that even political philistines and amateurs should be able to understand it, of the dialectical relationship between politics and organization, between political line and organizational methods; fifth, a polite invitation to the Dutch leadership to express itself on these questions and to signify its future intentions with regard to participation in our movement. We decided (I believe correctly) not to go "over the heads" of the CC at the present time and to address ourselves to the membership. We merely say in the letter that we take it for granted that the CC will explain to its own membership the reasons for its fateful steps at our conference; and that if it does make this explanation, then it will surely have no objections to submitting to its membership also the other side of the story, such as is contained, for example, in your letter to the conference and in our (i.e., the IS) letter to the CC of the RASP. If the CC *refuses* to accept this elementary proposal for an intelligent discussion in the ranks, then we have the right to consider which ways and means are best adapted to reaching the membership of the RSAP without receiving the kind permission of their CC, and thus breaking down the blockade that has been established between the international movement and the Dutch party membership. We have a big advantage, it seems to me, in the fact that the CC will find it politically impossible to consummate a break with us at the present time, although Sneevliet's line leads, objectively, straight in that direction (objectively and perhaps even subjectively; I must confess that he made a highly unfavorable impression on me especially at the conference, not of a revolutionary politician but of a disdainful bureaucrat with a revolutionary past). The time left for us in Holland must be utilized to strengthen all possible points of support, so that if and when a break comes with the CC, we shall not be in the tragic position in which we found ourselves under similar circumstances in Spain.[3]

Vereecken: he was completely isolated at the conference, although he tried to find some basis of a rapprochement with both Sneevliet and Molinier, as well as with Muste. But when he took his scandalous position with regard to the Molinier case,[4] I was forced to make a sharp attack on him. Muste had insisted on putting V. on the General Council or the [International] Bureau, and to avoid an additional struggle, we agreed; but after my attack on V.'s disgraceful unprincipledness, it was Muste himself who proposed that V.'s name be withdrawn from the list of candidates; so that V. was not elected on any of the three international bodies. So far as the record is concerned, by the way, Vereecken left his vote unqualifiedly (!) in favor of the list proposed by me in the name of the Org Com [organization commission].

Molinier: here too, except for Vereecken, we had no difficulty and the vote was therefore quasi-unanimous. I had another talk with Molinier and told him that so far as I was concerned, his readmission into the International was an open question provided that he showed in the next period (six months–one year) that he would not engage in or encourage any activities against our French section. Otherwise, we would have to crush any movement he sought to set afoot. I believe it made an impression on him, for he wants above all to do his work in *our* ranks. Whether he will conduct himself properly or not remains to be seen of course; but it is not vitally important. His movement is dead and the events will only reduce it further. Your letter about his possible displacement to the U.S. came too late for me to act upon it (day before my departure from Paris), but I do not exclude it as a possibility. I originally proposed it in Paris to the IS, even before the conference and the visit to Weksal; on second thought I found the idea a bit far-fetched; but I still do not believe it is entirely out of the question. If the French comrades agree, I can take it up with our comrades here, and then we can put the question to Molinier. I am inclined to believe he would accept such a proposition, because he hinted at it the last time we had a private talk together.

Muste: Your fears were groundless. He did try to play the conciliator with Sneevliet, but the conduct of the latter and our own conciliatory position left no room for an "independent" position. But while Muste gave us needless admonitions about the need of "understanding" the Dutch situation and of "proceeding intelligently," he did not take a position against that adopted by the conference. He confined his differences on the Dutch question to remarks about "shortcomings on both sides" which, I regret, did not illuminate the situation very greatly. As to the question of Abern,[5] I am very sorry that you agreed to Muste's written proposal. Fortunately, Muste did not propose Abern for the IS at any point during the conference or any of its commissions or in any personal conversation. I say "fortunately" because I would have been compelled to fight openly against it. Our CC has no *personal confidence* in Abern, who is so utterly factional in his dealings that he cannot even be trusted with confidential material which has nothing whatever to do with a factional fight. However that may be, the question did not arise at the conference and consequently no difficulties were connected with it. The list for the General Council, the Bureau and IS were unanimously prepared

3. This refers to the fact that when the Spanish section broke with the ICL to found the POUM and take it into the People's Front in 1936, virtually the entire membership of the section was lost for the ICL and the movement for the Fourth International in Spain had to be started over again from scratch.

4. Georges Vereecken voted against the conference decision to endorse the recent expulsion of Raymond Molinier from the French section and to prohibit political or organizational collaboration with Molinier by any member of the movement.

5. Muste had suggested Abern for election to the new IS at the conference, and Trotsky accepted the suggestion and recommended it to Shachtman in a letter on the eve of the conference.

and unanimously adopted (Muste and I finally "merged" our two proposals in the Org Com; I agreed to this because the differences in the two proposals were, after all, not decisive and certainly any concession made was a trifle in comparison with the value of averting "minority report"). Nor did we have any difficulties with the American resolution endorsing the entry. With one absolutely insignificant editorial change, the resolution was *unanimously* adopted, Muste also voting in favor of it.

As for my return to Brussels to work in the IS: Since my arrival in New York yesterday, I have only had the chance of speaking a few brief words with [Arne] Swabeck. He is entirely in favor of my going back. What the others will say I do not yet know but I think the prospects are fairly good that in a month or two I shall be able to leave New York again for a prolonged stay in Europe.

As soon as I have found my bearings here, I shall write about how matters stand with us in the SP.

Meanwhile, warmest regards to you and Natalia Ivanovna [Sedova] from my wife and me, and best greetings to the remarkable Knudsens.

Cordially,
Max Shachtman

Appendix C
Trotsky's Position in 1936[1]

Copies of the currently available correspondence in 1936 by Trotsky and the people who worked most closely with him in organizing and carrying through the international conference in July leave no room for doubt: he did not propose to the delegates that they should found the Fourth International at the July conference and they did not reject this proposal that was not made. What remains is to indicate what Trotsky did have to say on the subject in the period before the conference.

The Open Letter for the Fourth International, which Trotsky wrote in the spring of 1935 and which was published in the summer of 1935, briefly recalled "the struggle for its principles and ideas" since 1933 and said, "All this labor will indubitably proceed much better if correlated and unified on a world scale under the banner of the Fourth International." And it added, "The tempo and the time of the new revolutionary construction and its consummation depend, obviously, upon the general course of the class struggle, the future victories and defeats of the proletariat. Marxists, however, are not fatalists. They do not unload upon the 'historical process' those very tasks which the historical process has posed before them. The initiative of a conscious minority, a scientific program, bold and ceaseless agitation in the name of clearly formulated aims, merciless criticism of all ambiguity—those are some of the most important factors for the victory of the proletariat."

This open letter was the link that led to the July 1936 conference. It shows that in 1935 Trotsky had an open and flexible attitude on the whole question. He saw the tempo and timing of the new International as dependent on the evolution of the class struggle, but noted that this in no way relieved the Marxists of their responsibilities in the construction of the new International. He did not even mention a "proclamation" or "founding" of the Fourth International.

In February 1936 Trotsky was visited by two members of the American section, Maurice Spector and Lyman Paine. Most of their discussion concerned a proposal that the members of the Workers Party should join the American Socialist Party, which was approved later that month by a Workers Party convention. Toward the end of the transcript, Spector asked, "How do you conceive the main stages in the development of the Fourth International?"

After citing recent developments in Belgium and France, Trotsky said, "Nothing has changed. As I wrote to Muste and Cannon at the time of the Open Letter, I looked on it [the collaboration with Muste] as a lifelong alliance. I do not know at what stage the Fourth will arrive. Nobody knows. It is possible that we will have to enter again into a unified International with the Second and Third. It is impossible to consider the fate of the Fourth International apart from the fate of the national sections and vice versa. . . . If we consider the Fourth International only as an international 'firm' which compels us to remain independent propagandistic societies under any conditions, we are lost. No, the Fourth International is a program, a strategy, an international leadership nucleus."[2]

There is still no reference of any kind to "proclaiming" or "founding." The statement that the Fourth International is "a program, a strategy, an international leadership nucleus" might perhaps be interpreted to mean that the Fourth International already existed, since the program, strategy and international nucleus also existed. But it should be noted that this statement comes a little after the one where Trotsky said he didn't know, and "nobody knows," when the Fourth International would "arrive."

Trotsky and the IS agreed in April 1936 that the international conference should be held in the summer. In April he also began corresponding with Victor Serge in Belgium. Serge was one of the early Left Oppositionists in the USSR, for which he was brutally victimized. The Stalin regime finally permitted him to leave the USSR with his family in the spring of 1936, after protest campaigns by French intellectuals and the ICL. Years of banishment, harassment and isolation had caused Serge to lose touch with the thinking of the Left Opposition and the ICL, and to revive some of the syndicalist and anarchist sympathies of his youth. Despite this, Trotsky wrote him frequently in the spring and summer of 1936 in an effort to win him over politically to the ICL and to find a place in it for the literary contributions Serge was capable of making. One of the Serge letters, dated May 23 or May 27, 1936, which unfortunately was not available when the correspondence was printed in France,[3] must have asked Trotsky

1. The first generally correct discussion of this question that I have seen anywhere was by Pierre Broué, editorial director of the Trotsky *Oeuvres* being published by the Leon Trotsky Institute in Paris. See the interview with him in the French magazine, *Critique communiste*, no. 25, November 1978. But a later article by Broué ("Trotsky and the Proletarian Revolution of the Twentieth Century," in *La Verité*, no. 588, September 1979) unfortunately recycles the Frankian legend.

2. See *Supplement, Writings of Leon Trotsky*.

3. See *La lutte contre le stalinisme* (Francois Maspero, Paris, 1977), edited by Michel Dreyfus. All of the Trotsky letters to Serge are translated in *Supplement, Writings of Leon Trotsky*.

about perspectives or plans for the Fourth International. Trotsky's answer on this point, dated June 3, 1936, said:

"7. The Fourth International: I confess I do not understand what 'founding' the Fourth International means. There exist in different countries organizations and groups that struggle under this banner. They try to determine together their position on all the world events. They are preparing a common program based on practical and theoretical concepts rooted in history. Some Ryazanov[4] of the future may try at his leisure to resolve in retrospect the question of when exactly the Fourth International was founded. But as for us, we have simply to continue to develop our work."

When the Serge letter that Trotsky was answering is located, perhaps the significance of the reply will be clearer. Meanwhile here, for the first time in 1936 to our knowledge, Trotsky does refer to the "founding" of the Fourth International. But not in a favorable way. On the contrary, he takes a critical attitude to the idea, or at least dismisses its practical significance for the groups in different countries already struggling under the banner of the Fourth International. Future historians might have the leisure to figure out "when exactly" the Fourth International was founded, but the partisans of the Fourth International had more urgent things to do now.

The letter to Serge was sent only a month before Trotsky wrote the major resolutions presented to the international conference. He touched on the "foundation" question in one of these resolutions, "The New Revolutionary Upsurge and the Tasks of the Fourth International," which dealt with the massive strike wave in France and the opening of the civil war in Spain. Point 15 of this resolution said:

"15. Thus, all the tasks of the revolutionary struggle unfailingly lead to one task—the creation of a new, really revolutionary, leadership, capable of dealing with the tasks and possibilities of our epoch. Direct participation in the movement of the masses, bold class slogans taken to their conclusion, an independent banner, irreconcilability toward compromisers, mercilessness toward traitors—here lies the road of the Fourth International. It is both amusing and absurd to discuss whether it is yet time to 'found' it. An International is not 'founded' like a cooperative, but created in struggle. The June days [in France] provide an answer to the pedants who discuss its 'timeliness.' There is no room for further discussion."

Here Trotsky is concerned primarily with the "timeliness" factor. He calls it absurd to even discuss that factor after the recent upsurge of the French workers has demonstrated the need for a new revolutionary leadership. But he has something to add about the "founding" question: an International is not "founded" like a cooperative, but is created in struggle. (Whatever interpretation may be made of that, it is not the sort of statement that would have harmonized with a proposal for the conference to proclaim the founding of the new International.)

Another relevant point to be made about this and the other conference resolutions written by Trotsky is that in all of them he said, The Fourth International calls for this, the Fourth International stands for that, etc. In no place did his resolutions use the term "Movement for the Fourth International" which the delegates decided to adopt during the conference. This tends to support the probability that he never heard of the new name until after it had been adopted by the conference.

What do the various statements cited above suggest? The following, in my opinion:

We know of course that Trotsky wrote in 1935 and continued to believe until his death that building the Fourth International was the most important work of his life. Hundreds of letters and articles in 1935-36 express his conviction, publicly and privately, that the solution of the most crucial problems facing humanity in that period depended on the creation of a strong and effective Fourth International as soon as possible. Nobody disputes the fact that everything he did and said in 1936 was intended to hasten the creation of the Fourth International, and no interpretation of what he said about "founding" makes sense if it contradicts that fact.

But Trotsky did not equate the creation or bringing into existence of the Fourth International with its "proclamation" or "foundation." In fact, he distinguished between them rather strongly. Since he usually put quotation marks around "proclamation" and "founding," and then spoke about them with sarcasm or hostility, it seems to me that he attached some special meaning to those words. For him, those who spoke about "proclaiming" and "founding" had a concept of how to create a revolutionary International which he believed to be misleading and unhealthy, and he was trying to alert his comrades to beware of that concept and its consequences. *It can't be done,* he was saying, *by issuing a proclamation notifying the world that a new International exists; it can't be done through some formal act like taking a new name or passing a motion pledging to fulfill the functions of an International; no, it can only be done by continuing and intensifying the struggle for the International we began in 1933 and not letting ourselves be distracted by irrelevant or trifling pseudo-problems; the new International is timely now, but its arrival and success depend on hard work, not on useless or harmful "proclamation" and "foundation" formalities.*

This interpretation of Trotsky's position up to the 1936 conference is based, I must admit, on examination of only a part of the 1936 correspondence and documents. When the papers containing the letters to and from Trotsky are opened at Harvard in 1980, perhaps more light will be cast on the nature of the concepts that Trotsky was trying to counteract and how widespread they were in the ICL. Perhaps they will also disclose elements of a semantic problem. But I am certain that they will not show anything to support the legend of Trotsky proposing the founding or proclamation of the Fourth International in 1936. He simply did not see any point in such a thing in 1936, when he thought that without the formalities the movement should call itself the Fourth International, as he did in the resolutions he wrote for the conference.

I repeat "in 1936" because Trotsky changed his mind on this question in 1938.

For reasons stated in his letter of May 31, 1938, Trotsky disliked the name chosen by the July 1936 conference (MFI). But he was in complete agreement with the conference decision to set up a commission that would write a draft program; its final version (the "foundation document") was to be adopted early in 1937, after a four-month discussion, by the "first congress" of the Fourth International. Because the July conference was quickly followed by the first of the big Moscow trials, which compelled the MFI to concentrate all its energies on exposing the trials, this schedule was completely upset and the next conference was postponed a number of times before it was finally held in September 1938.

Did Trotsky see any contradiction between his remarks before the 1936 conference and the MFI's plans to prepare a "foundation document" for what we now call the founding conference or founding congress in 1938? We cannot say, but others in the MFI who worked most closely with him did not sense any inconsistency. Rudolf Klement is a good example. He was secretary of the July 1936 conference, and was administrative secretary of the IS until his murder two years later. In the latter post, it fell to him to write the IS circular-letter containing the formal call for the international conference in 1938. This first letter informing the national leaderships about the coming conference was dated April 1, 1938, less than two weeks after Trotsky's discussions with an

4. David Ryazanov, head of the Marx-Engels-Lenin Institute in Moscow in the 1920s, was in charge of research about the history of the revolutionary movement. Stalin purged him in the 1930s because he was an obstacle to the rewriting of Soviet history in the Stalinist mode.

SWP delegation about the conference. It was undoubtedly written in accord with Trotsky's views as Klement understood them, and he was better placed at the time to understand them than the other IS members. It is worth noting that Klement's letter referred to the coming gathering as the "Second International Conference for the Fourth International" (the official title of the July 1936 conference was the "First International Conference for the Fourth International"). Under this title he wrote:

"It is certainly not necessary to explain here the urgent necessity of this conference, in view both of the experiences lived through since the July 1936 conference and of the grandiose events to come. This will probably, in fact, be our last international conference before the outbreak of the world war and the revolutionary movements which it will inevitably engender. We must draw a balance sheet of our experience, verify, confirm and specify our program and our policies, consolidate the ideological and organizational bases of the Fourth International in order that it may effectively play the role that history has entrusted to it. Will it be a question of the 'foundation' of the Fourth International? This certainly is a poor way of posing the question. The process of the formation of the Fourth International commenced a long time ago and will not cease in the immediate future. It is necessary, in any case, that those who throughout the world are fighting for the Bolshevik program of the Fourth International should build, consolidate, enlarge their international organization, adopt, on the basis of their common program, common rules of conduct, apply on a national and international scale democratic centralism. May the Second International Conference be an important new step in this direction!"[5]

It is plain from this that at least echoes of Trotsky's 1936 views on "founding" were still reverberating at the time that the plans for the founding conference were being communicated to the leaders of the national sections in April 1938. There are even traces to be found in the last chapter of the transitional program, which Trotsky completed in the same month of April 1938. Polemicizing against skeptics asking if the time had yet arrived to proclaim the foundation of the Fourth International, Trotsky replied that it "has no need of being 'proclaimed.' It exists and it fights. Is it weak? Yes, its ranks are not numerous because it is still young. They are as yet chiefly cadres. But these cadres are pledges for the future. Outside of these cadres there does not exist a single revolutionary current on this planet meriting the name. If our International is still weak in numbers, it is strong in doctrine, program, tradition, in the incomparable tempering of its cadres."

But the name used in the conference call (the "Second International Conference for the Fourth International") was abandoned soon after it was introduced, along with the implication that the 1938 conference would not do anything essentially different from the 1936 conference. And despite Trotsky's April 1938 denial that the Fourth International needed to be "proclaimed," it was proclaimed at the 1938 conference, and its formal founding was incorporated into the statutes of the new World Party of Socialist Revolution.

Trotsky did not oppose these steps; in fact, he contributed to them heavily by his letter of May 31, 1938. There he explained that the name chosen in 1936 (Movement "for" the Fourth International) was being seized on by elements inside the movement to oppose or delay the creation of a disciplined revolutionary International. The resulting "indecision and lack of self-confidence" could do great damage to the movement; it was necessary to check the vacillators and backsliders in the most unambiguous way. While his letter only reiterated the thought he had in 1936—that we are the Fourth International and that is what we should call ourselves—it had the effect of separating the real Fourth Internationalists from the phonies and of reinforcing the trend toward "proclamation" and "founding" formalities at the 1938 conference.

To fully understand what Trotsky meant—in 1936, 1938, or any other time after 1933—it is not always sufficient to read what he wrote or said. Sometimes it is also necessary to learn what the other leaders of the movement were thinking, saying, worrying about or trying to do. Almost everything he wrote, including most of his public articles and books, was aimed at educating and consolidating an international cadre capable of the teamwork and discipline needed to build the Fourth International. Maybe Trotsky didn't always get the most accurate reports on what his fellow leaders were thinking, but he always took this question seriously and it affected both what he wrote and how he wrote it. Since Trotsky was in general one of the clearest of writers, an examination of what his comrades were thinking is recommended whenever there is any uncertainty or ambiguity about what he was saying and trying to say.

G.B.
August 1979

5. See excerpts from this circular-letter in *Cahiers Leon Trotsky*, no. 1, January 1979.

The US rulers' political crisis and working people's response

Are they rich because they're smart?

Class, privilege, and learning under capitalism

JACK BARNES

$10. Also in Spanish, French, and Farsi.

The Clintons' anti-working-class record

Why Washington fears working people

JACK BARNES

$10. Also in Spanish, French, and Farsi.

Is socialist revolution in the US possible?

A necessary debate among working people

MARY-ALICE WATERS

$10. Also in Spanish, French, and Farsi.

"When we face new and unexpected challenges we will always be able to recall the epic of Angola with gratitude, because without Angola we would not be as strong as we are today."

–Raúl Castro
May 1991

Cuba and Angola: The war for freedom

HARRY VILLEGAS ("POMBO")

$10. Also in Spanish.

Our history is still being written

The story of three Chinese Cuban generals in the Cuban Revolution

ARMANDO CHOY, GUSTAVO CHUI, MOISÉS SÍO WONG, MARY-ALICE WATERS

$17. Also in Spanish, Farsi, and Chinese.

ALSO FROM PATHFINDER

Malcolm X, Black Liberation, and the Road to Workers Power

JACK BARNES

Drawing lessons from a century and a half of struggle, this book helps us understand why it is the revolutionary conquest of power by the working class that will make possible the final battle against class exploitation and racist oppression and open the way to a world based on human solidarity. A socialist world. $20. Also in Spanish, French, Farsi, Arabic, and Greek.

Socialism on Trial

Testimony at Minneapolis Sedition Trial

JAMES P. CANNON

The revolutionary program of the working class, as presented in response to frame-up charges of "seditious conspiracy" in 1941, on the eve of US entry into World War II. The defendants were leaders of the Minneapolis labor movement and the Socialist Workers Party. Includes Cannon's answer to ultraleft critics. $16. Also in Spanish, French, and Farsi.

Trade Unions in the Epoch of Imperialist Decay

LEON TROTSKY, FARRELL DOBBS, KARL MARX

Food for thought—and action—from revolutionary leaders of three different generations of the modern working-class movement. Invaluable to the practical education of militant workers relearning today what a strike is and how it can be fought and won. $16

Counter-Mobilization

A strategy to fight racist and fascist attacks

FARRELL DOBBS

A discussion on strategy and tactics in the fight against fascist attacks on the labor movement, drawing on the experiences of the Minneapolis Teamsters movement of the 1930s. $8

Selected Articles on the Labor Movement

FARRELL DOBBS

"Militant workers need both a clear program and a sound strategy. Central to that fight is to politically arm workers to carry the class struggle to the governmental plane by creating their own political party."

—*Farrell Dobbs*

Articles from the *Militant*, written in the mid-1960s. $5

50 Years of Covert Operations in the US

Washington's political police and the American working class

LARRY SEIGLE, FARRELL DOBBS, STEVE CLARK

How class-conscious workers have fought against the drive to build the "national security" state essential to maintaining capitalist rule. $12. Also in Spanish and Farsi.

The History of American Trotskyism, 1928–38

Report of a participant

JAMES P. CANNON

"Trotskyism is not a new movement, a new doctrine," Cannon says, "but the restoration, the revival of genuine Marxism as it was expounded and practiced in the Russian Revolution and in the early days of the Communist International." Talks by a founding leader of American communism on building a proletarian party in the United States. $22. Also in Spanish and French.

EXPAND YOUR REVOLUTIONARY LIBRARY

Malcolm X Talks to Young People

"The young generation of whites, Blacks, browns, whatever else there is—you're living at a time of revolution," Malcolm said in December 1964. "And I for one will join in with anyone, I don't care what color you are, as long as you want to change this miserable condition that exists on this earth." Four talks and an interview given to young people in the last months of Malcolm's life. $15. Also in Spanish, French, Farsi, and Greek.

Lenin's Final Fight

Speeches and Writings, 1922–23

V.I. LENIN

In 1922 and 1923, V.I. Lenin, central leader of the world's first socialist revolution, waged what was to be his last political battle—one that was lost following his death. At stake was whether that revolution, and the international movement it led, would remain on the proletarian course that had brought workers and peasants to power in October 1917. $20. Also in Spanish and Greek.

"It's the Poor Who Face the Savagery of the US 'Justice' System"

The Cuban Five talk about their lives within the US working class

From police to courts to prisons to parole: how the US "justice" system works as "an enormous machine for grinding people up." Five Cuban revolutionaries—framed up by the US government and incarcerated for 16 years—draw on their own experience to explain the human devastation wrought by capitalist "justice." And what makes socialist Cuba different. $15. Also in Spanish, Farsi, and Greek.

Thomas Sankara Speaks

The Burkina Faso Revolution, 1983–87

In 1983 the peasants and workers of Burkina Faso established a popular revolutionary government and began to combat the colonial legacy of hunger, illiteracy, and economic backwardness. Thomas Sankara, who led that struggle, explains the example set for Africa and the world. $24. Also in French.

The Communist Manifesto

KARL MARX AND FREDERICK ENGELS

Why communism is not a set of preconceived principles but the line of march of the working class toward power, "springing from an existing class struggle, a historical movement going on under our very eyes." The founding document of the modern revolutionary workers movement. $5. Also in Spanish, French, Farsi, and Arabic.

Cosmetics, Fashions, and the Exploitation of Women

JOSEPH HANSEN, EVELYN REED, MARY-ALICE WATERS

How big business plays on women's second-class status and economic insecurities to market cosmetics and rake in profits. And how the entry of millions of women into the workforce has irreversibly changed relations between women and men—for the better. $15. Also in Spanish and Farsi.

U.S. Imperialism Has Lost the Cold War

JACK BARNES

The collapse of regimes across Eastern Europe and the USSR claiming to be communist did not mean workers and farmers there had been crushed. In today's sharpening capitalist conflicts and wars, these toilers are an intractable obstacle to the profit system's advance, gaining leadership experience as they fight. In *New International* no. 11. $16. Also in Spanish, French, Farsi, and Greek.

Teamster Bureaucracy

FARRELL DOBBS

How the rank-and-file Teamsters leadership in the upper Midwest organized to oppose World War II, racism, and government efforts—backed by the international officialdom of the AFL, the CIO, and the Teamsters—to gag class-struggle-minded workers. $19. Also in Spanish.

Letters from Prison

JAMES P. CANNON

The prison letters of a communist leader, jailed for his party's opposition to the US imperialist war effort in World War II. Cannon discusses organizing a revolutionary party in wartime and preparing its postwar political course. $25

Coal Miners on Strike

FROM THE PAGES OF THE *MILITANT*

The story of two battles by the United Mine Workers miners that pushed back efforts by the coal bosses and government to bust the union and reverse gains in eradicating black lung disease. What the 111-day 1977–78 strike and 72-day 1981 strike "showed above all else," say the authors, "is the power the working class of this country really has." $7

The History of the Russian Revolution

LEON TROTSKY

The social, economic, and political dynamics of the first victorious socialist revolution as told by one of its central leaders. How, under Lenin's leadership, the Bolshevik Party led millions of workers and farmers to overthrow the state power of the landlords and capitalists in 1917 and bring to power a government that advanced their class interests at home and worldwide. Unabridged, 3 vols. in one. $38. Also in French and Russian.

To See the Dawn

Baku, 1920—First Congress of the Peoples of the East

How can peasants and workers in the colonial world achieve freedom from imperialist exploitation? By what means can working people overcome divisions incited by their national ruling classes and act together for their common class interests? These questions were addressed by 2,000 delegates to the 1920 Congress of the Peoples of the East. $24

Workers of the World and Oppressed Peoples, Unite!

Proceedings and documents of the Second Congress, 1920

The debate among delegates from 37 countries takes up key questions of working-class strategy and program and offers a vivid portrait of social struggles in the era of the October Revolution. 2 vol. set. $65

Lenin's Struggle for a Revolutionary International

Documents, 1907–1916; The preparatory years

The debate among revolutionary working-class leaders, including V.I. Lenin and Leon Trotsky, on a socialist response to World War I. $38

Revolutionary Continuity

Marxist leadership in the United States

FARRELL DOBBS

"Successive generations of proletarian revolutionists have participated in the movements of the working class and its allies and sought to steer them along the correct path. . . . Marxists today owe them not only homage for their deeds. We also have a duty to learn where they went wrong as well as what they did right so their errors are not repeated."

—*Farrell Dobbs*

2 volumes: *The Early Years, 1848–1917,* $16; *Birth of the Communist Movement, 1918–1922,* $16.

Cuba and the Coming American Revolution

JACK BARNES

This is a book about the struggles of working people in the imperialist heartland, the youth attracted to them, and the example set by the Cuban people that revolution is not only necessary—it can be made. It is about the class struggle in the US, where the revolutionary capacities of workers and farmers are today as utterly discounted by the ruling powers as were those of the Cuban toilers. And just as wrongly. $10. Also in Spanish, French, and Farsi.

Episodes of the Cuban Revolutionary War, 1956–58

ERNESTO CHE GUEVARA

A firsthand account of political events and military campaigns that culminated in the January 1959 popular insurrection that overthrew the US-backed dictatorship in Cuba. With clarity and humor, Guevara describes his own political education. He explains how the struggle transformed the men and women of the Rebel Army and July 26 Movement, opening the door to the first socialist revolution in the Americas. $30

Aldabonazo

Inside the Cuban Revolutionary Underground 1952–58

ARMANDO HART

In this account by a historic leader of the Cuban Revolution, we meet men and women who led the urban underground in the fight against the brutal US-backed tyranny in the 1950s. Together with their comrades-in-arms in the Rebel Army, they not only overthrew the dictatorship. Their revolutionary actions and example worldwide changed the history of the 20th century—and the century to come. $25. Also in Spanish.

Women in Cuba: The Making of a Revolution within the Revolution

VILMA ESPÍN, ASELA DE LOS SANTOS, YOLANDA FERRER

The integration of women into the ranks and leadership of the Cuban Revolution was inseparably intertwined with the proletarian course of the revolution from the start. This is the story of that revolution and how it transformed the women and men who made it. $20. Also in Spanish and Greek.

Problems of Women's Liberation

EVELYN REED

Six articles explore the social and economic roots of women's oppression from prehistoric society to modern capitalism and point the road forward to emancipation. $15. Also in Farsi and Greek.

How Far We Slaves Have Come!

South Africa and Cuba in today's world

NELSON MANDELA, FIDEL CASTRO

Cuban internationalists "made a contribution to African independence, freedom, and justice, unparalleled for its principles and selfless character," said Nelson Mandela, speaking in Cuba in July 1991 alongside Fidel Castro. Here are their speeches on the victory by Cuban, Angolan, and Namibian combatants over the US-backed South African army that had invaded Angola. $10. Also in Spanish and Farsi.